AF342381

PUBLIC MANAGEMENT RESEARCH

PUBLIC MANAGEMENT RESEARCH
A Guide to
Research Capability Development

By

DONALD B. TWEEDY, M.A.

Principal Consultant (Ret.), The Diebold Group, Inc.
Scholar in Residence, Wilkes College
Wilkes-Barre, Pennsylvania

CHARLES C THOMAS • PUBLISHER
Springfield • Illinois • U.S.A.

Published and Distributed Throughout the World by

CHARLES C THOMAS • PUBLISHER
2600 South First Street
Springfield, Illinois 62717, U.S.A.

ISBN 0-398-04481-3

Library of Congress Catalog Card Number: 81-397

*With THOMAS BOOKS careful attention is given to all details of manufacturing and
design. It is the Publisher's desire to present books that are satisfactory as to their physical
qualities and artistic possibilities and appropriate for their particular use. THOMAS
BOOKS will be true to those laws of quality that assure a good name and good will.*

Library of Congress Cataloging in Publication Data

Tweedy, Donald B.
    Public management research.

    Includes index.
    1. Policy sciences—Research. I. Title.
H62.T84   350'.00072   81-397
ISBN 0-398-04481-3   AACR1

Printed in the United States of America
(PS-RX-1)

TO JESSIE

INTRODUCTION

W HILE IT HAS been said *all* knowledge may be of ultimate value in the solution of government problems, this guide is concerned with the organization and operation of those elements of *applied social research*, hereafter referred to generically as *public management research*, that are conducted by specialized organizational entities created for the following purposes:

1. accumulating, cataloging, analyzing, publicizing, and storing all kinds of public management information that may be of interest to the governments they serve
2. fulfilling research assignments on topics of interest to the officials of those governments and the public they serve
3. providing, as an auxiliary function, training in the methods and use of public management research

Research organizations intended to fulfill these needs are referred to here as Public Management Research Centers (PMRCs), although they are also variously known by names such as legislative reference bureaus, departments of governmental research, taxpayer leagues, bureaus of public administration, and research offices. The PMRCs discussed here are not concerned with research and development in the industrial sense, although much of what is discussed is equally applicable to both basic research and the kinds of invention, experimentation, and product development work conducted by some of the same kinds of organizations.

This guide will be useful to government officials and researchers at all levels because there is a discouraging lack of published information on public management research program organization and methodology. Most in-house libraries and governmental research programs were not designed, but rather, were started from unorganized and usually modest beginnings. They developed more in an effort to keep pace with the demands made upon them than as a result of a studied effort to plan for long-term growth in their scope and in the extent of their research services role. There is also little printed information for use in career counseling that adequately reveals either what a potential public management researcher should expect, if he elects to specialize in this increasingly useful and prestigious profession, or what qualifications he should possess.

Public managers are often called upon to undertake research projects other than studies of organization structures, methods, and procedures. They should, therefore, have the capability to do so with aplomb. For example, a public manager may be asked to research the extent to which a unit of government has found short-wave radio communications between its vehicles and the central dispatch office economical, reliable, and productive of faster service.

Another situation in which a public manager frequently needs help is when a government organization decides to establish its own research program, such as when a department of public health decides to set up a public health planning center. In that case, the appropriate official should be able to contribute to the design of the new center, the selection of managerial and technical staff, and in appropriate circumstances, show how existing resources can be utilized in the new project rather than duplicating them in a new center.

Initials are used liberally in this guide as abbreviations of organizational names and subjects. In instances where this is done, the name is generally spelled out the first time it appears in the text, with initials in parentheses immediately following. From that point, in general, only the initials are used. The following abbreviations appear with somewhat monotonous frequency:

1. PMRC which means Public Management Research Center
2. PMR which means Public Management Researcher
3. RS which means Research Sponsor or *client*
4. T/R which means Terms of Reference *Statement*
5. M&P which means Methods and Procedures studies

Citations to those reference sources which are specifically mentioned appear as footnotes. In this connection, it should also be pointed out that much, but by no means all, of the information in this guide is the result of actual experience, the author's and others, although originality cannot be claimed for all the ideas covered.

The first illustration in chapter 1 appears on the page immediately following the page in the text on which it is first mentioned. The rest of the illustrations follow this format.

The guide is divided into eight chapters that cover the essential aspects of designing a Public Management Research Center; the research project concept; the data gathering process in which library resources, field surveys and intraorganizational studies are employed; research reporting; and, finally, techniques for evaluating research programs and those who perform research tasks. The practical value of the material and its many illustrations have been tested by the author through their use in graduate teaching, consulting practice, and in-service training in the United States and abroad.

In the course of compiling this guide, the author was at first inclined to include both descriptions and reference citations to library and other research resources. This was urged on the theory that bibliographic guidance is often needed by governmental agencies in establishing their own in-house research capability. They also need to know what is available for immediate acquisition, what directories should be accessible to guide their employees, how to conserve their time, and when they must go to other libraries. The idea was also considered of including citations to a variety of guides to public management reference material in nonlibrary collections, such as public record archives, and in the records of organizations of public officials. In the interest of fulfilling the main purpose of this guide, however, attention is confined in chapter 3 to a summary of the types of research resources generally available, or which can be acquired, when the purpose and extent of a government's research program have been defined. Should the researcher in the field of public management wish to consult a reliable reference tool for the titles and publishers of the principal library resources, he should secure a copy of Anthony E. Simpson's *Guide to Library Research in Public Administration*.[1]

Most of the terms used in this text are self-explanatory in their context. It is, however, worthwhile to draw attention to certain terms used frequently, and especially subject to differences in meaning as a result of uncommon usage. In

---

[1]Simpson, Anthony E.: *Guide to Library Research in Public Administration*. New York, Center for Productive Public Management, John Jay College of Criminal Justice, 1976.

some disciplines it is not customary to refer to public officials as managers. Nevertheless, this is done deliberately here because all officials in public and public-oriented organizations are usually involved in activities such as production, supervision, provision of public services, and planning that are concerned with management in one way or another. Additionally, the more those responsible for raising levels of operational and research performance appreciate their management implications, the more effective their efforts are likely to be.

Administration is usually used here to identify the policy-making function, and *management* is used to identify the implementation of policy through action programs. These terms are used here synonymously because they interact so extensively. Where it is important to separate the policy-making responsibility, this is done by emphasizing the level of authority involved, or the program-wide implications of a decision on the results of specific research.

Organization refers to *any government establishment* created to achieve predetermined goals through the use of all manner of resources available for the purpose. An organization may be of any size. If size is a critical consideration, however, quantification in terms of the number of employees, the particular clientele served, or its geographic jurisdiction is indicated.

The terms *study, survey, investigation,* and *project* are used interchangeably. They all mean an approved assignment to apply research capabilities to the problems and activities of the entity requesting research assistance. For lack of more accustomed terms, *research sponsor* is used to mean that entity. When a limited number of people or an organization are especially concerned with the results of a specific program, they are collectively designated as its *clientele.*

ACKNOWLEDGMENTS

I T IS DIFFICULT to decide, in making acknowledgments, where to draw the line between one's own knowledge and experience, and one's debt to the advice and published work of others. This is particularly true when the experience was acquired over a number of years and in several developing countries, as well as at home. All the ideas and methods discussed in the guide have been tested on numerous consulting assignments and in collegiate teaching.

There are two professionals, however, who have been of direct assistance both through their editorship of comprehensive works in the field and their liberal expenditure of time for discussion during the progress of this work. One is Carl Heyel, a colleague while in the employ of the Diebold Group, Inc., in New York, and editor of *The Encyclopedia of Management*. The other is Dr. Archie M. Palmer, editor of *Research Centers Directory*.

A special word of thanks is due to Robert S. Capin, President of Wilkes College, and to the Management Dean, Dr. Andrew Shaw, Jr., who generously provided me with comfortable and convenient work space. And last, but not least, my gratitude to the head librarian, Dale A. Buehler and his staff, for their unfailing assistance and cooperation.

D.B.T.

CONTENTS

PUBLIC MANAGEMENT RESEARCH

Chapter 1

THE ORGANIZATION AND MISSION OF PUBLIC MANAGEMENT RESEARCH CENTERS

A CONSIDERABLE VARIETY of research is going on at university libraries, laboratories, or in the field. It is, and always has been, considered an essential element of an effective higher education program. This is particularly true of institutions, because it is necessary for the faculty to keep abreast of advances in their fields. Students are encouraged to participate in meaningful research projects, to develop an attitude of inquiry, to acquire a knowledge of research resources and techniques, and to learn how research findings can be most effectively communicated.

Since the mid-1930s especially, there has been a profound growth in the number of nonprofit organizations involved in carrying out research programs, the subject matter of which is in some way related to government, especially the management of public programs. To illustrate, there are at present well over six hundred research centers that are in some way concerned with public management research. Many of these research centers are affiliated with universities and taxpayer associations. If, however, the centers affiliated with governments and, therefore, devoted extensively to government managerial affairs were enumerated (which they have not been), the total would certainly exceed two thousand. This figure is estimated on the basis of the 1978 (6th) edition of *The Research Center Directory*, edited by Archie M. Palmer, Gale Research Company, Detroit. This directory excludes research *support* services such as computer centers, statistical laboratories, survey units, information retrieval facilities, research co-ordination offices, and those government internship and academic programs and institutions in which public management is an incidental concern.

The number and identity of the research centers is of superficial interest in comparison with the extent to which research has become an increasingly professionalized activity with expanding degrees of specialization knowing no geographic, sexual, or organizational affiliation barriers. Research programs relying upon governmental grants-in-aid and contracts with the United States Government, state and regional agencies, foundations, industrial associations, taxpayer groups and individuals have not been immune from the effects of financial retrenchment since the early 1970s.

In spite of the retrenchment that has occurred, however, the organizational structure, activity programs, and attraction of government-related research work to career-minded individuals have remained much as they have been since the mid-1930s. Like any other public or private organization, a PMRC cannot sustain very long its credibility without a clear definition of organization structure and the policies that provide the guidelines for carrying out its information gathering, storage, analysis, and reporting missions. The remaining topics of this initial chapter are devoted to how PMRCs most often originate, how they are organized, the conventional cycle through which research assignments progress, and guidance concerning a proven research project planning process.

HOW PUBLIC MANAGEMENT RESEARCH CENTERS ORIGINATE

A survey of governmental information and research organizations operated in one or more of the social sciences revealed no recognizable pattern of formation and growth. There are, however, common characteristics that provide some guidance to those faced with the responsibility of organizing a new PMRC.

Suggestions by Administrative Officials

The decision to create a separate research center most often has its roots in suggestions by one or more public managers or individuals serving on the policy-making body of the organization. These suggestions are often prompted by the frustration experienced in the decision-making process because of the lack of sufficient or appropriate information concerning on-going government programs and projects. This is especially true with respect to new programs or the expansion of programs to include new activities or an enlarged clientele.

Suggestions by Senior Executives

When the decision has been made that a public management research capability be developed, it is often for the same reasons as attributed to policy-makers. In recent years, however, there has been an increasing tendency for managerial officials at all levels of government to express their need for more and better information for use in making *operating* decisions and in improving their ability to respond promptly with facts and recommendations when called upon by those at the policy-making level of government and by members of the public.

Suggestions by Outside Organizations and Individuals

Taxpayer organizations, in particular, have developed their own information resources but have found their search for current and comprehensive data on public management matters in their jurisdictions very difficult. Many such organizations have encouraged governments to become both the repositories of operating data and a prime mover in the interpretation of that data through the employment of researchers, statisticians, accountants, lawyers, and other specialists in the social sciences disciplines.

Suggestions by Associations

Associations of businessmen or professionals in various fields have, as an adjunct to their clearinghouse, training, and activity programs sponsorship, urged supplementing their own research work with the establishment of interorganization government research programs, such as surveys, economic trend data collection, and the publication of journals that contain articles, reports, digests, book reviews, etc., of interest to their members.

Suggestions by Legislative Committees and Commissions

State and local governments that use the committee system under which specialization in particular facets of the policy-making function is assigned for fact-finding purposes also employ personnel from disciplines such as law, accounting, personnel management, and statistics either on a full-time basis or on an as-needed basis to research the problems upon which members must vote. These special purpose policy development organizations have often become valuable information resources. When they have become generally recognized as offering an excellent way to expedite the decision-making process, they tend to proliferate. This has led to a recommendation that they be consolidated into what are variously called *legislative reference bureaus, research centers, investigation units,* or similar descriptive names.

Once the determination is made to centralize or to embark on an in-house government research capability, the matter of how the new activity shall be organized becomes critically important.

PMRC ORGANIZATION

There is no consistent organization pattern followed by the designers of existing PMRCs, nor is there any consistency in what the heads of PMRCs say they would do along organizational lines if they were to restructure the programs they head. There are mixed views, for example, on whether responsibility for directing a PMRC should be under the wing of the chief executive officer of the parent organization or should be considered to be so in need of impartiality and integrity that responsibility for its policies and resources should be guided by a legislative committee or a special commission created by the legislative body.

In both governmental and business research programs there are marked preferences for the director to report to the chief executive officer of the parent organization. Mainly in professional and trade organizations, in which there is a more pronounced desire to spread managerial responsibility over a wide membership base, *research committees* take their place among other organizational committees, such as those dealing with membership, organization development, program, budget, library, or entertainment. All of them usually report to or are appointed by an elected governing board with little chance of change in their composition except through attrition.

The *Conceptual Organization Chart—Public Management Research Center* illustrates a fairly conventional organization structure, based on *functional* considerations, such as the separation of managerial affairs from the center's library, research, overall direction, and fiscal affairs. The differences between the organization structure illustrated here and an organization pattern that would apply to a PMRC serving a smaller government organization is that there would be a doubling up of functional responsibilities with primary emphasis on the recruitment of researchers, a librarian, and a stenographer. The addition of other research support personnel would then be timed to conform to the volume of research assignments, and the extent to which the center's services are expanded to include responding to routine inquiries and assisting other organization elements to prepare and produce reports.

PMRC STAFFING PATTERN

PMRC staffing depends mainly on the amount of financial support available and the scope of the research program. Furthermore, what is called for at the outset of the PMRC's existence is sometimes quite unlike what evolves thereafter. If its program is a success from inception, it is likely to have the approval of those it serves manifested in widespread support for a larger staff, more space, improved information retrieval systems, and better ways to communicate its findings and to implement the results of its information analysis and research work. If there is a significant lack of funds, however, program development is retarded, especially in terms of qualified staff, which invariably represents the greatest single classification of expense.

Depending on the size of the research staff, the work of the PMRC is usually divided to reflect specializations. It is generally the practice, however, to regard all professional researchers as *generalists* even to the extent of expecting those with specialist qualifications to work on assignments that may not have any or very little use for their specialized capabilities.

In recent years, leadership and key roles in PMRCs have centered on social scientists, mainly drawn from the academic community, irrespective of whether the program concerned has been entirely government oriented or not. Formal training for the PMRC managerial role is not provided in college curriculums; therefore, research directorships are usually filled by promotion from within the program, transfers of research-inclined operating officials to this activity, or by recruiting outside the organization for an experienced director. This clearly suggests that there is no more managerial difference between industrial enterprises and a governmental undertaking than there is between, for example, the innumerable kinds of industrial enterprises that engage in research and other development activities.

The *Conceptual Organization Chart—PMRC* illustrates the wide selection of managerial research, analysis, and financial and overall direction activities required, as well as those logistic and production activities usually found in a typical PMRC. The principal difference between them is size, which, as previously indicated, is almost always a function of the amount of funding available to provide the kinds and number of specialist personnel needed to augment the generalists, and support personnel who carry the main research support load of the center.

It is generally agreed that all managerial, analyst, research, and support positions in the PMRC should be subject to written *job descriptions* in order that incumbents may have a clear understanding of their responsibilities, types of duties to be performed, and what employment standards apply. A *Sample Job Description—Staff Supervisor of Research* is provided here mainly to illustrate the format and content of a typical job description that covers the job definition, duties, and standards that might be applied to a staff supervisor of research. A brief discussion of the several areas of functional responsibility in a typical PMRC also follows.

CONCEPTUAL ORGANIZATION CHART
PUBLIC MANAGEMENT RESEARCH CENTER

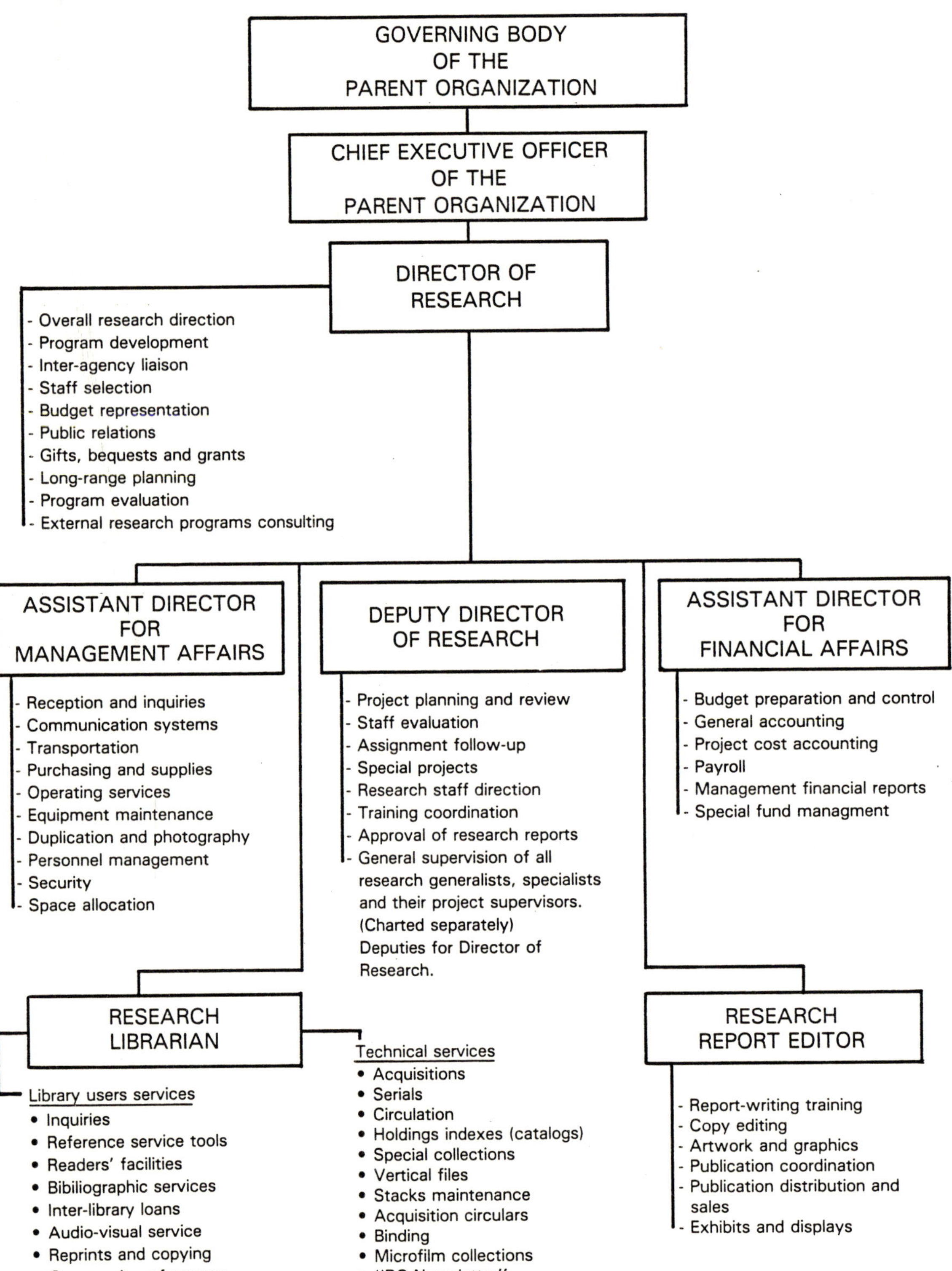

STAFF SUPERVISOR OF RESEARCH

DEFINITION

Under general direction of the Deputy Director of Research, plans, directs, and organizes research and analysis activities of a special research project team engaged in the collection of a variety of operations, statistics, and other data; supervises a staff of professional and technical personnel in implementing a major program of research activity; and does related work as required.

EXAMPLES OF DUTIES

Develops necessary forms and written instructions for research project reporting necessary for statistical accountability, statistical reporting, and research purposes; makes detailed analyses and interpretations of collected data; writes analytical narrative reports and descriptive summaries; compiles and prepares reports and project program studies for publication; develops sample surveys and research projects necessary to evaluate quality and effects of program activities, to determine specific characteristics, or to obtain specific information not normally reported or available; interprets statistical data for Director and Research Center staff and in response to organization inquiries; participates in group meetings and helps prepare interpretational and educational material for the research center and the public; meets with representatives of other agencies in gathering and analyzing operating statistical and fiscal data; prepares reports and studies required by organization regulations; presents data in graphic, tabular, and written form; and may direct preliminary planning and preparation of material for data processing.

EMPLOYMENT STANDARDS

Any combination of education and experience equivalent to graduation from college with courses in statistics and four years of progressively responsible experience in professional statistical or research work, including one year of supervisory experience in work related to the Government Research Center.

Director of Research

The senior leadership position in a PMRC is variously called director of research, research bureau chief, or research department manager or chairman. In some situations, this official may be involved in the overall organization activity of the governmental agency so that his title may be enlarged to encompass this often prestigious responsibility. For convenience, the first listed title, *director of research*, is used in this guide.

Managerial practices vary considerably between PMRCs with respect to managerial style and the policies promulgated for the guidance of the center's staff and the clientele that it serves. They depend mainly on the managerial and leadership characteristics of the director and usually reflect the need for his or her direct participation in all or most of the center's activities, the need for coordination between the functional elements of the center, and the extent to which the director's time and energies must be devoted to outside contacts, such as the promotion of the use of the center and relations with the public.

In general, the director of research should be expected to carry two main kinds of responsibility. The first of these is to meet *staff* (personnel) needs, and the second is to meet *organizational* (program) needs.

Staff and Individual Needs

Staff and individual needs about which the director of research should be constantly aware relate mainly to conditions of employment and to the fulfillment of career-related opportunities. The following are among the most important and frequent subjects about which PMRC staff members appear to be concerned.

SATISFYING WORK is the most critically important element for professional people, especially researchers. It is not particularly difficult to meet this need in PMRCs that develop their own programs, but when the program is dictated by specifications from the center's clientele, this may become somewhat difficult because satisfaction in research often comes mainly from a sense of developing one's own ideas. If assignments are too constrained from the outside, an important value to the individual researcher is lost. Furthermore, a highly centralized heirarchy within the PMRC that preempts the main decisions to itself may have the same stifling effect on creativity. In such situations, the staff become *processors* rather than *creators*.

Awareness of this personal need is the first step to overcoming the barriers involved. The director must, among other things, withdraw as far as possible from the *conduct* of assignments once the *Terms of Reference Statement* (T/R) has been approved and the answers to questions on who is to do what have been developed. This implies a degree of confidence in the abilities of the personnel involved, which leaves decisions on the day-to-day handling of assignments to them. This does not mean, however, that the director of research should relinquish the observation of work, although most of this, too, can be delegated to the appropriate supervisor.

PERFORMANCE INFORMATION FEEDBACK. The essential elements of a performance feedback system designed to give support to research effort are quite simple. They can be summarized to include the following:

1. Identification of expected accomplishments in the light of previously defined missions, responsibilities, and duties.
2. Explanation of the requirements of each accomplishment. If there are any doubts that the researcher understands the reasons why an accomplishment and its requirements are important, these must be explained fully.
3. Description and illustration of how performance will be measured and why the measurement criteria have been selected.
4. Setting of exemplary performance standards (i.e. worthy of emulation), preferably in both quantitative and qualitative terms.
5. Identification of exemplary performers and any resources that researchers can employ to become exemplary performers.
6. Introduction of frequent and unequivocable feedback about how well each researcher is performing. This confirmation of performance is best expressed as a comparison with an exemplary standard, with the consequences of good and poor performance made clear.
7. Provision of as much helpful backup information as possible (and needed), to help researchers troubleshoot their own performance and that of the researchers for whom they are responsible.
8. In all cases, an attempt to relate the various aspects of unsatisfactory performance to specific remedial actions.

Even though the foregoing elements of a performance feedback system are simple and easy to initiate, their usefulness requires very systematic care and analysis. The effects of a good performance information feedback system that meets the above requirements can be extensive. There are exceptions, however, such as situations in which those being evaluated have not been trained adequately. When this condition prevails, the feedback of performance data is not apt to have as extensive an effect. It follows, therefore, that it is critically important for researchers to know *how to perform* and how to *know when they are performing well*. Experience in evaluating research performance has clearly demonstrated that in developing a public management research team, the *confirmation of performance* weighs far more heavily in the achievement of high performance than does the training provided in research methodology and bibliographic skill and analysis.

PROFESSIONAL RECOGNITION. Professional recognition is strongly motivated by a desire for favorable reactions to achievement by one's organizational associates, as well as that which arises from invitations to appear at professional meetings, publication of research findings and conclusions, and participation in prestigious academic and/or professional associations.

While professional recognition cannot be entirely controlled by a PMRC director, experience has demonstrated that the extent to which a staff member is *encouraged* to accept opportunities to display his capability and actual achievements under favorable circumstances is an important motivator and effective indicator of leadership support. This is especially important to the more junior members of the staff. Among the ways to start the process is to provide *exposure* within the organization served by the center through attendance at appropriate interdepartmental meetings and conferences on subjects of particular interest and by encouraging joint authorship of journal and newsletter articles and commentaries on the work of others.

GROUP IDENTIFICATION. Group identification is a greater need in some individuals than others; therefore, the response to it varies accordingly. Those who elect government research as a career are more likely to react positively to group identification than those who, for example, have more introspective personalities and, therefore, tend to be less responsive to the stimulation that comes from animated discussions of observations and conclusions.

It is not particularly difficult to satisfy the need for group identification. It can become difficult, however, in situations in which the center staff is split into factions competing for budget allowances or seeking any of the other types of advantages found in service-oriented activities. It is the research director's responsibility to establish PMRC-wide goals concerning research progress and its end results. It has been amply demonstrated in many types of organizations that the satisfaction of working with respected associates and the sharing of achievement/recognition accrues to the individual staff members virtually as a natural outgrowth of group effort and group life.

It is also part of the director's challenge to make a clear distinction in his/her behavior between those managerial tactics which increase the psychological benefit of group identification and those conditions which might prevent their natural and spontaneous development. Factors such as personal jealousies, favoritism, unreasonable discrepancies in salaries, special privileges, and indecisiveness or vacillation in policies are likely to foster disunity and thereby prevent the kind and level of group identification that most researchers require.

EQUITABLE FINANCIAL AND STATUS REWARDS. Financial and status rewards are needs that can be separated but should not be accommodated through differing tactics. To illustrate, financial gain is not the *primary* incentive that attracts people to research. As people who live on salaries, however, they cannot very well afford to be entirely indifferent to the economic returns of their positions. A director of research, therefore, has a continuing responsibility to evaluate the contribution of each of his staff and, within the limits of his authority, to adjust their remuneration and rank accordingly.

Adjustments in salary and rank include insuring parity between elements of the organization as a whole as well as with other elements of the organization and with outside organizations. It also includes seeing that budgetary allocations are sufficient to effect promotions. While the director may not have unrestricted latitude in effecting adjustments in individual ranks and salaries, the first step should be to present a strong case for a budget allocation sufficient to permit flexibility to forestall resignations in situations in which the reason is mainly inadequate remuneration.

RESEARCH ENVIRONMENT. A satisfactory research environment is seldom as important to an individual researcher as the other factors described previously, but it can sometimes have a negative effect on performance. Cases in point are inadequate furnishings; lack of equipment; overcrowding; inordinate distances between work areas and the usual office amenities; badly controlled comfort conditions, such as heating, lighting, cooling, and the contamination of the atmosphere with noise, odors, dust, and other natural and man-made disturbances.

The director's responsibility in accommodating all of these needs is to support the staff in such a way as to make their efforts efficient and effective—*efficient* in accomplishment with the least expenditure of money and effort, and *effective* in the achievement of objectives most fully and individually rewarding.

Organizational Needs

Just as individual members of the PMRC have personal needs that influence their contribution to organizational goals and any recognition they receive, so are there organizational needs that must be accommodated.

ORGANIZING A PMRC. Organizing a PMRC is like organizing most other service-oriented programs in which a variety of capabilities are brought together to achieve a common set of goals. In the context of a PMRC, organization entails the bringing together of talented people, and assigning to them individually and collectively certain responsibilities in order to achieve the following objectives:

1. Provide the director with sufficient freedom to handle those activities that are implicit in his/her leadership role that he/she cannot delegate to others.
2. Bring the director into a close working relationship with his/her principal associates in a way that permits a sharing of authority for major policy decisions and helps in performing the many and various managerial functions for which he/she is responsible.
3. Delegate to individual research teams a large measure of discretionary authority for fulfilling assignments with a minimum of overhead direction and day-to-day supervision.
4. Provide a workable device whereby the intermediate and junior members of the staff may become involved in the development of organizational policy without being involved in major commitments of PMRC time and broad managerial considerations.
5. Foster a center-wide attitude of common purpose and loyalty.
6. Establish appropriate policies and the machinery for implementing longer-range programs of recruitment, training, and other forms of staff development.
7. Make provision for the representation of the

center before the organizational hierarchy, the service or profession to which the center is related or of which it is an integral part (public and professional organizations), and the media through which the public is informed of the center's goals and achievements.

PLANNING. Planning is vitally important to the long-range development of a PMRC program. It is usually quite difficult to describe except in very general terms. It is possible, and not usually particularly difficult, however, to *plot a general course* for the PMRC, with clear definitions of parameters and with some flexibility in the forecast of the rate of progress.

Predictions of this type invariably depend on the sufficiency and clarity of the perceptions of the center's basic mission and goal in order that specific plan-related decisions may be seen as either relevant or, alternatively, as not being applicable to the staff and the PMRC's parent organization. If they are specifically relevant to the PMRC staff, additional considerations, such as flexibility, organizational growth, the impact of possible governmental changes, new or increased emphasis on what and how organizational services are produced and delivered need to be carefully assessed in the development of both short- and long-range organizational plans. The genius of successful planning is said to lie in knowing when to pursue a steady course and when and how to avoid the impact of a storm.

COORDINATION. Coordination in research work has been defined as the actions necessary to regulate and combine for effective and harmonious group performance. Coordinating the various elements of a PMRC organization is by definition a responsibility of leadership. It does not, however, necessarily mean *dictation*. This is because the effectiveness of group performance in matters such as research often calls for participation by many persons on an essentially equal basis.

In a PMRC situation, the principal objective of internal coordination is to achieve effective and equitable production; *effective* in the sense that the different parts of the effort reinforce rather than frustrate each other; and *equitable* in the sense that organizational policies apply realistically and evenly throughout the PMRC and the overall organization of which it is a part. This coordination is also a function of leadership. The challenge is for the PMRC to give more effective support to the parent organization and to receive an equitable level of support from it.

The director of research will usually find that most

of his/her coordination effort is spent within the PMRC and will be in the form of consultations with the heads of various PMRC elements on matters of priority, the cost-benefit of alternative courses of action, assignment of extra-research and extra-analysis support activities, evaluation of individual and team performance with a view to remuneration and rank adjustments, and responding to the need for PMRC-wide participation in policy decisions.

The main focus of coordination in a PMRC is the production of the ultimate product, i.e. information analysis and research. A satisfactory production record is usually the consequence of many persons' efforts. It follows, therefore, that everyone in the PMRC carries some share of responsibility for getting its work accomplished. There is, however, an overriding obligation carried by those in managerial positions to see that the center as a whole is productive.

While research productivity is difficult to define and even more difficult to measure with precision, some form of *program evaluation* must be evolved and applied if the center is to have a workable personnel policy and be in a position to estimate its progress toward fulfilling its mission and program goals. Chapter 8 deals with the evaluation of the PMRC program as a whole, and the capability of its researchers. The sum total of these evaluations can be accepted as an accurate, though admittedly quite subjective, assessment of PMRC production, capability, and performance.

CONTROLLING. Controlling should not be confused with any of the above described organizational needs. It is simple in context but often quite difficult in application. In context, it is merely the periodic assessment of the results of a program in the light of the *planning* that took place earlier, and then taking whatever action is necessary to *correct* deficiencies that caused lack of assignment fulfillment or any other evidence of noncompliance or underproduction. The evaluation tool provided in chapter 8 will assist in that endeavor.

Generalist Researchers

Generalist researchers usually compose at least 65 percent of a PMRC staff. Like most other professional and paraprofessional positions in large governmental organizations, a generic (overall) title is usually applied with a qualifying adjective, such as *principal*, *associate*, *senior*, or *junior*. This sort of designation is generally used in connection with salary allocation and is often supplemented by the use of a working title such as *project manager*, which may be assigned to anyone who is put in charge of a specific research or survey project. It is also sometimes used to designate anyone who has a continuing responsibility for all work within a special area. If the PMRC is sufficiently large to justify two or more professional research *teams* or *groups*, for supervision purposes, the senior official of each is usually called by a working title, such as *section chief* or *section supervisor*.

Specialist Researchers

Whether or not full-time specialists are employed, the research staff should not be considered as fully capable unless there are team members (sometimes called coordinators) who can be assigned overall responsibility for at least the following phases of the PMRC's work:

1. *Economic researcher specialists* who are sometimes selected on the basis of a combination of economics and statistical research capabilities. The *Sample Job Description—Economic Research Specialist* is typical. It may be used as a model in drafting position specifications for other researcher specialties.
2. *Legal researcher* who should provide opinions on the legality (statutory as well as judicial precedents and administrative regulations) of existing or proposed courses of action, research

and draft proposed legislative enactments, prepare testimony in connection with court proceedings, etc.
3. *Methods researcher* who makes organization and methods studies or contributes technical skill to assignments carried out mainly by generalist researchers.
4. *Engineering researcher* who covers the mechanical, civil, and electronic engineering skills. The main requirement here is to have a continuously available technician who can prescribe and interpret engineering requirements.
5. *Financial researcher* with specialized knowledge of fiscal matters such as budgeting, long-range financing, cost-benefit analysis, financial service contracts, revenue sharing, internal auditing methods and procedures, etc.

ECONOMIC RESEARCH SPECIALIST

DEFINITION

Under direction, to do major economic studies including data collection, analysis, and forecasting; and to do related work as required.

This is the full professional level position in the economic researcher specialist series. It differs from lower level economic researcher positions in that it applies the full range of economic analysis techniques to assess and report on segments of the economy. Supervision is normally limited to statements of objectives and review of work of lower level economic researchers through periodic conferences and the evaluation of reports.

EXAMPLES OF DUTIES

Collects, organizes, analyzes, and interprets economic data; prepares reports of findings; investigates and develops statistical series, economic models, and other measuring devices; makes projections and forecasts concerning segments of the economy; conducts market research including evaluating potential markets, quality control, packaging, distribution, and related factors; evaluates effect of government and industrial economic programs.

EMPLOYMENT STANDARDS

Any combination of education and experience equivalent to graduation from college in economics; at least four years of increasingly responsible work in an administrative capacity where economic data was utilized in program planning and/or program evaluation assignments; and two years of professional research experience.

6. *Automated data processing systems analyst,* including analysis and research capability in determining the feasibility of computerizing operating procedures and the usual alternatives to this technology, such as employing accounting machines and other less sophisticated mechanical processes.

It bears repeating that if it is not financially or otherwise possible to employ full-time specialists in the previously mentioned or any other specialties, the alternatives of staff sharing, secondment from the organization's line and staff activities, or employing specialists on a part-time or an as needed basis may be feasible.

Professional and General Research Support

Except in very small PMRCs, certain types of specialization are usually provided by fully qualified journeymen who can apply their skills in almost any kind of organization. To provide maximum *support* in a PMRC program, some civil service experience is necessary and a lot easier to acquire than the research skills employed. It is not usually practical to have the following categories of specialists divide their time between their specialty and generalist information and research work, although they should be considered important resource persons in the fulfillment of those types of research which call for their specialized capability.

Reference Library Services

A reference library and a systematic way to catalog and retrieve information are PMRC *musts*. In organizations in which the research activity is sufficiently well-funded to permit a reference library either as a supplement to, or instead of, a reference facility for organization-wide use, a professional librarian should be a high priority staff addition.

The librarian should be fully qualified by training and experience in the management of a *special library* or, alternatively, if recruited from a general library, be provided with the opportunity to secure appropriate formal training and to visit established PMRC libraries to observe the handling of the many functions expected of librarians and their specialized subordinates. The *Sample Job Description—Chief Research Librarian* is typical.

It should be expected that anyone within the organization who has a scholarly interest in specialized knowledge, especially new information in their professional or avocational field, will make known any findings (citations) that will increase the research resources of the center.

This means there should be at least one person on the PMRC staff assigned the task of communicating the center's desire to have recommendations on relevant publications or other informational resources. It does not follow that everything suggested should be immediately acquired for the center's library, but rather that those who accept the responsibility for being on the lookout for resource material should provide a complete and accurate citation that can at least be entered in a card catalog.

It should be the duty of the librarian, whatever the title and whether a full-time assignment or not, to see that the citations are evaluated and, if found appropriate, cataloged either in the general reference card file or in a special card file maintained for references to items that are not (yet) available in the center's library collection but that might be borrowed through a union of libraries.

It will save a great deal of time and duplication of effort, such as having to make follow-up requests for more complete or accurate citations, if each person who undertakes the lookout work is given appropriate instruction in the preparation of index cards. It should also be the librarian's duty to refer to the usual informational sources for book reviews and other book selection aids in reaching a recommendation on what printed material should be acquired for the center or by any other locally accessible library.

In the design of the classification and cataloging system, provision should be made for making the transfer of research reference material, citations, extracts, and synopses covering books, pamphlets, journals, abstracts, etc., easily transcribable to computer input media. Sooner than was generally expected, PMRCs have found it necessary to install standard operating procedures under which they participate (through the use of remote computer terminals) in interlibrary data storage and retrieval systems. This is already being done in many technologies; therefore, it is best to anticipate the more widespread use of computers for information retrieval purposes in public management.

It should be the assigned duty of one or more members of the library staff to cull all incoming publications, especially professional journals and other serials in search of articles, book reviews, conferences, university sponsored lectures, etc., in

Sample Job Description

CHIEF RESEARCH LIBRARIAN

DEFINITION

Under general administrative direction of the Director of Research, plans, organizes and manages the Research Center Library; manages any government grants-in-aid to libraries; provides consultative library service to other organizations' libraries; and does related work as required.

EXAMPLES OF DUTIES

Manages the Research Center Library; formulates library plans and policies subject to the review of the Director of Research; and determines financial needs; prepares the budget and supervises the expenditure of funds allocated; directs the selection, organization, and training of the library staff; manages grants-in-aid to libraries; advises and works in the establishment of other research libraries; establishes book collections; furnishes consultative services on library management, classification, and book acquisition to other organizations; directs the keeping of necessary records, statistics, and reports; advises on the establishment and operation of special libraries by other organizations and in the design of interlibrary loan, etc., services.

EMPLOYMENT STANDARDS

Any combination of education and experience equivalent to graduation from college; the appropriate graduate level course in librarianship generally required for the master's degree; three years of increasingly responsible employment in professional library work that included extensive contact with researchers in the social sciences.

order to bring them to the attention of interested members of the PMRC professional staff. Various methods of circularizing the staff are in present use. Photocopying processes are generally available so that the quick duplication of printed materials makes it unnecessary to cut articles from journals or to circulate the complete publication.

Controllership

Controllership service on a professional level is needed, because it is often necessary to provide timely and accurate cost information relative to past and anticipated research projects. Occasionally, general accounting, purchasing, etc., services are provided by a centralized financial activity for an entire government organization, but it is usually necessary to supplement the information received with more detailed information on aspects of research projects such as generalist, specialist, and support activities, as well as the estimated contribution of client staff to assignment fulfillment. Such data cannot ordinarily be provided through a general accounting system, but with a relatively low level of additional input from the research staff in the form of cost breakdowns, this budget and cost analysis information can be produced more promptly and in the detail needed for planning and project control purposes.

Report Editorial Service

On a professional basis, report editorial service makes a great deal of difference to the acceptance of reports. All senior and most intermediate level researchers have considerable experience in expressing their thoughts in writing. This is not enough! A professional editor is able to contribute to the way research findings are expressed and organized in relation to a *theme* or *message*. Help should also be available with respect to the design of the report, and the illustrative material intended to support the findings and conclusions reached. Whether this service is provided through a full-time report editor, or on an as-needed basis, there should be no compromise on whether or not this support is made readily available.

General Services

Supervision is required over the maintenance and operation of the communication, duplication, custodial, equipment availability, clerical, stenograhic, drafting, artwork, security, and accident prevention services—the usual general services required in a PMRC. They are adequately identified in the Conceptual Organization Chart—PMRC.

Research Interns

Research interns are college-level students or recent graduates who, for pay, experience, or both, enter upon a transition experience from college-level learning to the real-life of the professional world. Public Management Internship programs are encouraged by academic institutions as well as governmental organizations mainly because fledgling researchers are afforded an opportunity to work with experienced professionals (usually called *mentors*) and to observe and assess the theories, skill requirements, and attitudes of these professionals. The main strength of the internship concept is found, however, in its power to develop a feel for the reality of analysis and research within a frame of reference that classroom lectures and postgraduate seminars cannot provide.

Chapter 2

PUBLIC MANAGEMENT RESEARCH
ASSIGNMENTS AND PROJECTS

BEFORE DISCUSSING the most important aspects of public management research projects, it is useful to consider an overview of their principal elements. The *Public Management Research Project Cycle* illustrates a typical research project from the source of the assignment to the postimplementation follow-up report. The elements in that cycle are discussed in this chapter.

SOURCES OF PUBLIC MANAGEMENT RESEARCH ASSIGNMENTS

Heads of government research centers generally contend they have a backlog of requests from departmental officials to undertake projects of immediate importance to their programs. It usually emerges, however, that most such centers have been in business for five years or more, and that their reputation for consistently satisfactory results is the cause of the backlog. During their first year, and sometimes for much longer periods, attention is focused on projects of interest to the organization as a whole and to the *public* it serves. For example, the gathering of data on population, employment, education, income, property ownership, housing, health, and public service needs is often undertaken without specific reference to which department or other suborganization will have immediate or even long-term use for the information. Once projects that are confined to the collection of such generally useful data have been initiated, they often become *continuing* research assignments for the center. After the initial *debugging* of the data-collecting and data-processing procedure, continuing research projects are usually carried forward by junior researchers and clerical personnel, either by way of field trips or by mail, and the results are set out in new or updated data tables and narrative statements.

Irrespective of how continuing assignments originate, they provide an important informational resource. So important, actually, that the establishment of a PMRC for gathering and interpreting census-type data may be cost beneficial as well as technically justified in view of the widespread use of such information and results.

Apart from continuing efforts, project assignments usually come from the following sources and in the approximate frequency in which they are summarized in the following subtopics.

The PMRC Itself as an Assignment Source

Observations made by researchers in the course of their assignments provide the most productive source of suggestions for additional research in the same or closely related areas. This happens so often that the question of priority must be reconciled with other research commitments. In order that the center's service image may be enhanced, it is best to discuss the need for *additional* work with the sponsoring organization before initiating the extension of an ongoing project.

Whether or not a project from within the center itself is immediately undertaken, it is highly desirable that those involved should promptly reduce their suggestion and any thoughts on what benefits will accrue to writing in order that it may be placed on the agenda for staff consideration and the assignment of a priority status.

The file of future research projects should be revised at least semiannually, if for no other reason than that it keeps the staff alert to subjects that have already been given serious preliminary consideration but have not yet been assigned a tentative start-up

THE PUBLIC MANAGEMENT RESEARCH PROJECT CYCLE

A. *Sources of Research Project Assignments* (in order of frequency)
- Research Center staff based on organization contacts, etc.
- Top management officials, including intra-organization referrals.
- Research sponsor(RS) organization's supervisory staff.
- RS organization's research needs committee.
- Boards of Directors and Councils of parent organizations.
- Other organizations such as professional associations, etc.

B. *The Project Planning Process*
- Research project conference with RS representatives.
- Development of Research *Terms of Reference Statement*(T/R).
- Selection of RS project liaison officer.
- Announcement of research assignment.
- Estimate of researcher and RS staff needs and selection of research team.
- Research team briefing on mission and individual assignments.
- Distribution of assignment/work schedule to concerned officials.

C. *Data Gathering Process*
- Collection of facts, including past reports, on all areas covered by the T/R.
- Recording through the use of narrative statements, schedules, charts, etc., data concerning the research assignment.
- Securing modification of the T/R if needed.
- Recording all tentative research conclusions and ideas.
- Submitting progress report to Director of Research and the RS liaison officer.

D. *Data Evaluation Process*
- Comparing collected data to combine and eliminate duplications.
- Conferring on preliminary conclusions and selecting those to be developed further (with alternatives wherever indicated).
- Refining conclusions and submitting to project team with appropriate supporting data, such as cost-benefit data, estimates of training/promotional needs, report publication costs, etc.
- Verifying all data to be used in the research report.
- Drafting tentative report on alternative conclusions.
- Modifying report draft to eliminate or clarify conclusions not considered good candidates for RS acceptance.
- Holding RS conference on conclusions and preparing final report giving appropriate attention to any RS objections or countersuggestions.

E. *Final Report Delivery and Implementation*
- Final report transmitted to appropriate RS official(s) by Director of Research in accordance with RS wishes.
- If an implementation plan *has been requested,* take steps to hold a conference with RS in attendance at which time the report is approved, partially approved or rejected and a plan for implementing the approved recommendation is discussed.
- Develop implementation schedule, select RS and research team members, etc., to carry out the implementation work.

F. *Research Report Follow-up Process*
- Within eighteen months of submitting the final report, contact RS liaison official concerning a review of implementation.

date. It also affords the opportunity to abandon or consolidate related project ideas in an effort to keep the research backlog within reasonable limits.

Organization Officials as Assignment Sources

The number of research project suggestions arising from staff meetings is about equal to those initiated by individuals. Those arising at staff meetings tend to deal more with *policy* matters of immediate urgency than as a result of current practice comparisons and long-range planning. Essentially the same occurs when public officials meet to discuss the introduction of new services, changes in the delivery of long-established services, and the extension of public service programs to a new or enlarged clientele. Such discussions almost invariably concern new insights and process adjustments that cannot usually be developed without further research.

The referral of an assignment emanating from senior management officials to a newly established PMRC is sometimes a slow process. The center must earn the confidence that comes only through satisfying its sponsors. Furthermore, managers who have not had the help of research centers are accustomed to making assignments to members of their own organization or to contracting it to consulting firms, trade associations with which they are affiliated, and research companies that specialize in the kinds of problems with which the manager in question is concerned. This is especially true if these arrangements have proven useful in the past or come well-recommended by acquaintances who have used them.

Research Sponsor Committees as Project Assignment Sources

This category of research project assignment sources is confined to organizations characterized by their large size, rapid growth, and the employment of new or rapidly changing technology. These characteristics make them prime movers for more research projects. Included here, although the same characterization need not always apply, are those organizations that use employee suggestion plans and welcome ideas that call for research either within the department or by a research center that serves the entire organization.

Government employee suggestions deal mainly with procedural improvements, service delivery changes, and ideas already in use. They usually represent *unofficial* and unsponsored individual research effort by employees actively engaged in the tasks to which their improvement ideas are related.

Ideas of value to the organization are usually rewarded with a cash payment in proportion to their value in terms of savings or service delivery benefits.

The journey from the *suggestion box* to approval and implementation is usually long. The existence of a departmental suggestion committee makes the route at least one step longer, but it has the advantage of encouraging more widespread participation by those at the lower levels of organizational authority and responsibility. In the interest of conserving its manpower and facilities, it is best for the PMRC not to become too actively involved in employee suggestion plans, except for the occasional review of suggestions as an idea evaluating resource. The real merit of employee suggestion plans is that they have an occasional idea that merits more complete research.

Boards of Directors and Councils as Assignment Sources

It is often difficult to identify the real source of research project assignment suggestions when they emanate from a public authority council. They may have started at any point between an employee suggestion and an expression of interest by a council member, or on the basis of an article read in a journal or a discussion with a friend. That they are recorded in the official minutes of the policy determining body provides all the incentive needed by a director of research to give prompt attention to drafting a plan of action or, alternatively, to preparing a brief against the assignment if that course of action appears to

him/her to be in the best interest of the PMRC program or the parent organization. There is no limit inwardly or outwardly to the size of research projects emanating from boards or councils. Many are assigned to PMRCs because it is not obvious to any of the members where the research should be undertaken.

A device that some research directors have found effective in avoiding excessively ambitious assignments from the top level of authority is to take steps to acquaint as many members of the council as possible with the work and limitations of the center through briefings and the delivery of copies of reports and periodic project progress summaries. Another control device is for the chairman of the policy body to exercise his/her authority to refer project assignment requests to the chief executive officer of the organization for his/her review prior to formal board or council action. In such situations, the chief executive officer will normally ask for the views of the director of research and any concerned department heads.

In the case of new PMRCs, it is well to include discussion of a project assignment suggestion in a meeting of those responsible for its origin. If the center encounters this problem at a later stage of its existence, it may be preferable to meet it head on by conferring with the chief executive officer and/or the chairman of the board or council on what strategy to employ.

Other Assignment Sources

Trade and professional associations are usually mentioned as *occasional* sources of research project suggestions. Many associations have developed their own, often extensive, research capability during recent years. Some are limited by the extent to which their findings must be shared within their membership indiscriminately, because their sources of information are sometimes inhibited by the need for confidentiality as to performance indicators, strategies, and other operational considerations. In situations in which an association is not able to maintain its own research capability, it is prone to call upon its membership for help in assessing suggestions; designing research projects; processing data received from participating members; and circulating copies of its findings, conclusions, and any recommendations. These are often on a confidential basis but may be subject to leaks to the press and to nonparticipating individuals or organizations.

The sources of project requests can best be summarized by stressing that the compelling considerations are the center's *reputation* amongst its prospective sponsors for high quality *results* and its ability to provide help beyond that which the sponsor can

provide for itself or secure through any professional or trade association affiliation.

It is of the greatest importance that, in the beginning, the center evaluates over a period of months the major problems its parent organization faces, and determines what course it will follow in screening these problems. To illustrate, where should the new problem-solving effort start? Will solutions come through meeting the need for an organization analysis, improving purchasing methods, mechanizing procedures, decentralizing or expanding the geographic areas served by all or certain elements of the government, diversifying service, introducing computer-assisted reporting, or what?

One particularly effective director of research expressed his advice in general, but instructive terms. His comment was that a new PMRC should *not take the big job first*. He went on to say that research centers are not born strong; they are born weak; they gather strength by successful projects so that they should creep before they walk and walk before they try to run. This advice suggests that a PMRC should begin with those activities or subjects that offer the greatest promise of a good showing, even if a modest return.

THE RESEARCH PROJECT PLANNING PROCESS

A large part of the success of a research project depends upon the effort put into its planning. Planing calls for a thorough assessment of the problem to be documented and the end result expected. This initial stage of project planning calls for recognition that public management research is an activity in many respects like manufacturing, selling, providing health services, or operating a computer center. It requires knowing what each aspect of the research mission is, for what the results will be used, and a realistic view of what resources must be utilized to achieve the expected research results.

Because research is almost always done for others, it is especially important to know in specific terms

what those who have requested the project really want. Depending mainly on the scope of the project, the planning process should fulfill all, or at least most, of the following objectives:

1. Require the preidentification and prescheduling of all project work
2. Ensure coordination among the organization units involved
3. Provide a record of officially approved goals
4. Permit forecasting of research results against actual progress that can be measured
5. Provide clear assignments of responsibility for achieving the expected results

Assignment Conference with the Research Sponsor

A relatively few public managers have difficulty in putting their ideas into writing, especially those ideas that call for action by others. Their communications ability sometimes fails, however, when they try to explain in detail exactly what is wrong with present situations and what should be done to correct them. In many cases, they also have neither the time nor the talent for analyzing conditions that are adversely affecting their areas of responsibility so that they are unable to point out exactly what help they need and how that help will solve their problems. It is necessary, therefore, for a representative of the PMRC to accept requests for research assistance in whatever form they are received and to decide which of the two following courses of action should be pursued:

1. Approach the RS at once to arrange a conference for the purpose of securing a more complete understanding of what is wanted.
2. Conduct a preliminary study of the subject matter mentioned in the RS request, whether it be a written memorandum, telephone call, a statement made in a conference, or a message passed along by a third party, such as a division head or the organization's chief executive officer; then arrange a conference with the RS for the purpose of clarifying any uncertain items or of proposing limitations within which the assignment can be undertaken.

Development of Research Terms of Reference Statement

Irrespective of which course is followed, the main thrust of a project conference should be to develop a concise statement of exactly what research effort is to be provided. This does not mean that the conclusions should be anticipated, but rather the areas to be researched should be *identified*, and what conclusions are to be *sought* should be sufficiently explicit to provide guidance on *goals* rather than the *route* to be taken. Any decision on route, i.e. methodology, should be reserved for the research team that undertakes the assignment.

Terms of Reference Statements

Terms of Reference Statements (T/Rs) are short, agreed-upon summaries that constitute the authority under which the PMRC is to conduct its assignment. As such, the T/R should always be reduced to writing in order to minimize misinterpretations and ambiguity. It should spell out what is expected and, in general terms, what RS organization resources (if any) are to be made available in carrying out the project. A standard format for such T/Rs is not practical in view of the great variety of projects undertaken. The following actually used T/R illustrates compliance with the general requirements of such a document:

To investigate, by observation and discussion with administrative, management and technical personnel, the condition of the office machines, equipment and furnishings in a representative cross-section of government organizations. To the extent that needs can be met through the application of *preventive maintenance* techniques, propose a program of organization-wide action, the purpose of which should be to eliminate work interruptions and the unneces-sary expense which results from breakdowns and damage to office equipment and furnishings.[1]

Alternatives are available as to when a T/R should be developed and agreed upon, but there is no disagreement as to the need for, and the purpose of, this important device for ensuring a meeting of minds on what is to be done by whom. Some PMRCs prefer that the RS making a research request provide such a statement at the outset and that it be the basis for any negotiations needed to clarify and formalize project objectives and participation. Others contend that it is premature to issue a T/R before a preliminary study has been made and that a statement based upon such a preliminary study will reflect what is to be done, what results are to be sought, and to whom the results are to be provided.

A third way to handle this matter is for either the RS or the center's representative to summarize any discussions that have occurred in a preliminary statement that, after RS study, can be modified as needs indicate. Such an agreed final statement can thereafter serve as the project T/R. Nevertheless, unexpected conditions are often encountered in the course of a project that prompt a meeting with the RS and a determination on whether the T/R should be amended to include a broadening or narrowing of its provisions. In all cases, modifications should be covered either by a written statement amending the original T/R or by memorandum in which the agreed

---

[1]Tweedy, Donald B.: *Report on a Proposed Furnishings and Equipment Preventive Maintenance Program for the Government of the Sudan.* Limited publication, 1976.

changes are fully explained. If the T/R is to be reviewed for amendment purposes after a preliminary study, a statement to that effect should be included, indicating who is to redraft it in the light of agreed-upon amendments.

A T/R may be quite narrow, dealing with a relatively small operating problem, or quite wide, such as that covered by the statement quoted previously on the preventive maintenance of office furnishings and equipment. Irrespective of the size of the assignment, its purpose should be specifically stated. The following are *typical statements* that clearly indicate project purposes that might be quoted individually or jointly in a T/R:

1. Determine needs for, and then provide, proposals on how to produce and make available to management, more, better, and faster information for decision-making purposes.
2. Apply clerical work study techniques to the purchasing department personnel in order to establish standard times for often repeated operations, to assist in allocating work, to control work assignments, and to determine the number of personnel required and what training activities are indicated.
3. Explore the feasibility of computerizing the principal record creating, record maintenance, and record storage work of the organization.
4. Strengthen operating procedures and controls for the protection and security of assets including furnishings, equipment, spare parts, cash, and evidence of ownership and debt.

There will be occasions when the RS has already reached tentative conclusions and wants their *confirmation*, a *better way* to reach present goals, or a *modification* in anticipation of technological breakthroughs that will have a serious impact on present practices. Unexpected conditions, such as a recent technological discovery or the publication of a highly authoritative monograph, open new avenues of research, prompt the dropping of all or part of an ongoing research assignment, or defer the research assignment until all concerned have a chance to consider the new development and to reassess needs. In all such cases, the already approved T/R should be amended in writing to cover the changes or deferment.

To summarize, the end result should be a T/R that serves as the basis for staff assignments, the marshalling of information and experimental resources, and the assignment of the project to a place in the center's work schedule.

Development of Project Plan and Staff Assignments

A *project plan* is a written description of a program of work developed to secure necessary executive approvals and to guide and control the personnel assigned to the project. Its main benefits are the following:

1. Forces *preplanning* and *prescheduling* of all research project work
2. Ensures *coordination* among the organizational units involved in fulfilling the project mission
3. Permits *forecasting* of staff accomplishments and, thereby, of overall progress and a completion date
4. Provides specific assignments of *responsibility* for each task and of *accountability* for the achievement of end results

The PMRC should also develop its own internal procedure for the preparation of project plans. While the format and the information contained may vary to meet specific requirements, the following topics should be covered, irrespective of their arrangement and the detail presented in each:

1. *Project (or assignment) title* should conform to the wording used in the RS request for assistance or, alternatively, the wording used in the T/R.
2. *The general approach to assignment fulfillment* is a step-by-step outline of how the project work will be carried out. It may mention the need for, and how, a preliminary survey of information resources will be conducted.
3. *Need for interim conferences* with, and reports to, the RS.
4. *Participation* by the RS, such as the temporary assignment of personnel and decision whether experimental work or a test run of proposed policies and procedures should be undertaken.
5. *An expected benefits statement* is mainly intended to focus attention on the justification for undertaking the project. It is a sound rule that information analysts and research projects should not be undertaken without a clear conception of expected benefits. The reasons why the RS asks for assistance may provide the key elements of an expected benefits statement, but the PMRC should not hesitate to draw attention to other benefits such as the project's expected social implications and the possible improvement in

the organization's community- or industry-wide image.

6. *The work schedule and staffing plan* is not only capable of being illustrated in chart form but should also include narrative detail, such as the identification of the principal tasks to be performed, the junctures at which RS personnel will be utilized, and conference dates with RS management personnel to review progress to date or the emergence of an unexpected problem.

7. *Approvals* should be expected from the hierarchy of the PMRC as well as the RC. After negotiations on the timing of inspections and the use of RS personnel, approval of the T/R may be a mere formality. If the names of those who are to approve it are provided, it gives the PMRC useful points of contact during the project work and specific guidance on who are the real sponsors or probable beneficiaries of the assignment.

Selection of RS Liaison Official

Depending on the scope of a project, and this may vary from project to project, the head of the organization requesting the project may wish to serve as his own liaison. Reasons may range from a desire for confidentiality to being certain that any publicity concerning it will give appropriate recognition to his role in the progress of the organization of which he is a part. Whatever the motives, the work of the center, during the planning and early stages of its project work, will be facilitated if the supervisor has just one point of reference when there is need for RS help or has someone with whom to discuss the procedure to follow in overcoming barriers or a proposed modification of the T/R. In the interest of operating efficiency, the RS liaison officer should be a fairly senior official of the organization, with authority equal to that of a deputy to the principal executive officer of the department concerned.

The qualifications of the RS liaison officer should include an extensive knowledge of the organization's mission and mode of operation. He should also be a person with widespread rapport and respect. Equally important to the success of the project is his knowledge of the project's T/R and a personal commitment to do all he can to acquaint those concerned with the project conclusions and the benefits that will accrue from the implementation of its recommendations.

From the outset of his representation assignment, it should be made clear that the liaison person is not a member of the project team, nor does he have final authority with respect to authorizing changes in the scope of the project work or its T/R. His principal concern is to expedite changes, when needed, by virtue of his ready access to the chief executive officer of the department. His advice is also invaluable on alternative courses of action and informational resources, and he is in a position to provide departmental services such as extra typing, duplicating, drafting, transportation, etc. He may occasionally be called upon to intervene on behalf of the PMRC, but this should be a rare occurrence. Whatever action appears necessary should always be assessed in terms of the relative importance of the expected project results, as well as the protection of the department from unnecessary and potentially damaging interruptions and/or intrusions.

Announcement of Research Project

In most situations, the publication of news about a pending research project is not necessary, and in some cases, it may not be in the best interest of its success. If the subject matter is of a confidential or security nature, it should not be publicized; steps should be taken to ensure that potential leaks are appropriately plugged, and precautions should be taken to protect the materials being used for unauthorized personnel and outsiders. This may mean providing intrusion-proof facilities, such as lockable files and work spaces and protected communication equipment.

In planning the publicity that may be wanted by the RS and acceptable to the research center, it should be borne in mind that a considerable amount of research, no matter how well planned and how well the research team is staffed, produces little or nothing of intrinsic value. Furthermore, predictions on findings and conclusions are subject to misinterpretation by those who have something to gain or fear from their effects, especially those which have not yet been researched. It is therefore preferable to withhold publicity on prospective research projects in which the elements of controversy, confidentiality, etc., are present. It should suffice to announce within the RS organization that the PMRC has been asked to carry out a project that may entail the use of records and other organizational resources and that all concerned are expected to make those resources available when requested. Announcements should include notice of the selection of the RS liaison official to whom RS personnel should direct questions or refer to secure authorization to provide data that is customarily considered confidential.

Estimate of Project Staff Requirements

The care taken in preparing a research plan will pay dividends in time saving as well as in being able to know at any time exactly where the project stands in terms of the expected and actual completion dates of all of its parts.

If the PMRC has two or more research assignments in progress at the same time, it may be difficult to utilize particular personnel for assignments that fit their specializations. In that situation, the supervisor must deploy the available staff to the best of his ability and rely upon *time-sharing* assignments, and occasional consultant-type participation by specialists to bolster those parts of the assignment in which there is a lack of full-time capability.

It should be a part of all project assignments to schedule completion on at least an approximate basis. Whether or not the precise completion date is indicated, the scheduling of staff time to the project should be done as a preliminary to final acceptance of the assignment and the drafting of the T/R. The allocation of individual time can be done in the light of ongoing projects and any extra project work to which members of the research team may be committed.

The total project effort can be broken down into time segments based upon *tasks* to be performed. While it may not be possible to schedule work exactly, it is always possible to identify and classify generally what is to be done and by whom. A worksheet entitled *Work Schedule* should be prepared for each research assignment. This form should be *headed* in essentially the same manner as the *Task List* and then vertically arranged in columns as follows:

1. Columns 1 and 2 (¼ inch and 2½ inches respectively) provide for the sequence number and the name of each activity to be performed.
2. Columns 3 through 28 (3/16 inch wide) provide for each successive five-day sequence of work periods within a particular series of work weeks. Shorter or longer work periods may be used as circumstances dictate.
3. A ¾ inch column on the far right edge of the form is provided for entering the total number of calendar days and man days devoted to each research activity. This data can be posted as a fraction, the numerator being the calendar days and the denominator being the aggregate man days of involvement with each activity.
4. Across the entire space devoted to five-day work periods should be noted the months in which the work is to be performed.

The appearance of the work schedule is that of a bar chart, with lines being drawn from the start to the scheduled completion of each research activity. Researcher names may be written on whichever *bars* apply to their assignments, along with the expected number of man days each researcher will be engaged in work relating to the activity concerned.

The use of a work schedule, which allows the posting of research team names as well as activities, can be scheduled with a high degree of realism. To illustrate, the following tasks are typically undertaken in research projects dealing with public management problems such as the quality of a particular government service:

1. Study of all available and acquired library material and organization records
2. Field investigation (if necessary), including visits to organizations where work on the subject field is in progress or has been done in the past
3. Analysis of findings and making decisions on tentative (thus far) conclusions
4. Progress report to the director of research and RS liaison officer, followed by RS conference
5. Development of alternative conclusions and/or solutions to problems encountered
6. Drafting of final report
7. RS conference on findings and conclusions, and if required, recommendations and proposal on a cooperative plan for implementing recommendations
8. Implementation assistance if requested
9. Solving unforeseen or unforeseeable problems
10. Follow-up evaluation inspections and conferences

Team Briefing on Project Mission and Assignments

In most situations, the briefing of the research team on its overall mission and individual assignments is mainly a review of the RS conferences that led to the adoption of the T/R, and a more detailed discussion of the tasks that project fulfillment will require. The work schedule will be found useful in identifying each staff assignment because it discloses to the team members what share of the project each person is to have and the time-frame for each task. It is usually beneficial for the RS liaison official to be present, and it will help to establish a working rapport

if he is asked to speak on what research resources, such as reports and records, are available within the organization he represents and who, in particular, should be consulted on matters of special relevance within the project's mission. He may also be able to discuss previous research efforts and the problems left unsolved for lack of staff, research materials, etc.

Distribution of Assignment/Work Schedule

It is often an important result of the above-mentioned team briefing that adjustments are made in the schedule and individual assignments. This is especially so when some team members are to work on a part-time basis. Regardless of whether or not adjustments are made, a copy of the work schedule

and staff assignments should be posted in the PMRC office, and copies provided to the RS liaison official, the director of research, and the records clerk of the PMRC, as a signal that the project has been launched, in order that an individual set of file folders may be readied for the orderly filing of all project records.

Chapter 3

THE DATA-GATHERING PROCESS— PUBLISHED RESEARCH RESOURCES

THE DATA-GATHERING process should not begin until a decision has been reached either to make or withhold a formal announcement that the project has been implemented. If an announcement is to be made, it should signal the actual launching of the data-gathering process. This signal may be in the form of a staff memorandum, directed to all employees of the activity centers concerned, posted on a bulletin board usually reserved for announcements of organization-wide or local interest, or a news story issued for publication in the organization's *house organ* or the public media. The choice of announcement medium and the amount of detail included in the story will depend upon the importance of the project and the degree of certainty of expected successful results.

The success of a public management research effort will vary greatly between projects. For example, the mission of a particular project may be to produce as much factual information on a subject as possible. It need not include the submission of recommendations on how to handle the problems disclosed, nor an interpretation of the data, for the reason that this may be the function (mission) of the organization that originated the project. It may be desirable to withhold announcement of the research effort until it is practically certain the results will be of considerable interest or sufficiently controversial so that a *progress report* type of announcement might serve to alert those concerned to anticipate with favor its potential results.

The data needed to fulfill research assignments varies greatly between subjects. The methods employed, however, are essentially the same whether the subject is a new management policy, a diversification proposal, a manpower utilization study, a public service need, or innumerable other subjects of concern to government organizations.

The most commonly employed public management resources in print are described in the topics that follow.

LIBRARY RESEARCH MATERIALS

Most research assignments start with a search for *documentation* on the subject under study. This usually takes the greatest amount of the researcher's time, but it provides the background so necessary to the successful employment of the methods described next.

The sources of printed material for research use are too varied and voluminous to identify in detail here. Every governmental organization should have the leading publications, books as well as journals, relating to its activities. Back numbers of journals should be indexed if this is not already done by the publishers and filed for future reference. Books, especially textbooks used for teaching and handbooks, which are usually devoted to technical treatments of unusual as well as more conventional forms of data and modes of operation, tend to get somewhat out-of-date within ten years and should be replaced as new publications are reviewed favorably by known authorities on their specializations.

During recent years, book literature in many fields has been augmented by the publication, usually by professional, trade, and scientific organizations, of their research and experimentation in *pamphlet* form. These pamphlets are frequently mentioned and sometimes reviewed in the new book section of technical journals and trade papers but are not usually cataloged either as books or as periodical articles.

The majority of reports or monographs produced by university research programs are much the same as the limited edition pamphlets, since they are not always mentioned in news stories, but they are sometimes mentioned in annual reports and in specialized technical journals, especially those published by universities. These research reports, articles, and pamphlets should be sought by either the PMRC, or the professional staff and the PMRC library acquisition personnel for indexing, cross-referencing, and bibliographic use. Suggestions on previously unknown sources of printed reports, technical papers, etc., also emerge in the course of interviews and the use of the more conventional research tools described in this chapter.

A *library research tool* is a publication that is consulted for specific information or for guidance on where to find information on a particular subject. The facts about information resources are brought together from a vast number of publications and then conveniently arranged and indexed for researcher use. The number and content of research tools increases each year and can generally be characterized as reflecting a trend toward greater interdisciplinary consideration of subjects, concern with international developments, recognition of many subspecializations within subjects that have traditionally been considered as standing alone, attention to informational accessibility, and, finally, a recognition that there have been new areas of knowledge resulting from the development of new technologies and research interests.

What follows is an introductory list of the *primary* research tools relating to the management of public organizations.

1. Encyclopedias and dictionaries
2. Library catalogs
3. Computerized reference data banks
4. Magazines, journals, and other serials
5. Books and pamphlets
6. Conference proceedings
7. Newspapers
8. Biographies
9. Bibliographies
10. Government publications
11. Archives and manuscripts
12. Almanacs, maps, atlases, gazetteers, and travel guidebooks
13. Photographic materials
14. Machine-readable records
15. Research-in-progress

It will be observed that the list of library research resources is headed by encyclopedias and dictionaries and that library catalogs are second on the list. These have been found to be the most useful at the outset of a public management research project. Computerized data banks occupy the third position because it is important for the researcher to become as familiar as possible in a short time with the main topics of interest in the research subject before starting to seek out the informational resources that will best meet his needs. It is altogether possible that, if the researcher has access to a computerized data bank, he will not need to utilize the other resource indexes for the development of his bibliography of reference materials. It is therefore most important that the researcher investigate thoroughly which computerized services are most suitable for his purpose in terms of coverage and cost. The services mentioned next, and those few which could not be described for lack of space in a monograph of this kind, are *research tools* for securing a *comprehensive bibliography on a narrowly defined topic*, not a *selective bibliography on a general subject* or broadly based topics within that subject.

Encyclopedias and Dictionaries

An encyclopedia has one principal purpose—to be a *basic* reference tool for the researcher who needs elaboration on a subject in which he is not an expert. The implication of basic is that an encyclopedia, while it is usually comprehensive in *breadth* of coverage cannot be comprehensive in the *depth* with which it treats most topics. Furthermore, an encyclopedia should direct the researcher to information at the next level of depth, through cross-references to other research material and a bibliography.

A *dictionary* is mainly a research tool that provides the correct and alternative *spellings* of words and an *explanation of their meaning*. Specialized dictionaries, such as the *Dictionary of Administration and Management*, by the Systems Research Institute Staff (of Los Angeles), sometimes go further by providing information on the derivation of words, and explanations that are virtually encyclopedic in their comprehensiveness.

Encyclopedias and dictionaries are by far the best places to start an information search because an important beginning can be made to understanding the overall scope and content of a research subject by reading a *systematic summary* by an expert. Encyclopedias usually contain condensed articles on many aspects of subjects. They are generally available in public libraries and are always available in college libraries. They are often available in business libraries and among the reference books in government organizations. The articles are written and updated periodically by known authorities in their fields and usually include pictures and statistical schedules to illustrate comparisons and trends. They are often kept current by annual yearbooks that deal with recent developments, important events, and personalities.

Library Catalogs

While much of the search for information relating to business and public management ideas and techniques will be devoted to sources other than books, library catalogs should be consulted early in that search, because they contain references to materials considered sufficiently important to merit special recognition whether in books or other published media. An often overlooked merit of library catalogs is the identification of textbooks that contain references to other published materials.

It is a tribute to practioners of library science during the past decades that public, academic, and most special libraries are organized on substantially the same basis. Their general reference card catalogs are usually arranged so that the researcher will have little difficulty in learning to use them in spite of minor differences.

The two principal differences the researcher will encounter are that the practice of maintaining a *general catalog* is surpassing the practice of having two separate catalogs, one for *author/title* cards and the other for *subject* cards. In a general catalog, the two identification systems are combined so that the user may proceed with a search in one catalog, knowing only the author's name or alternatively knowing only subject designations.

In addition to the general catalog, some libraries have a separate card file system, in which cards exactly like the author/title and subject cards are filed according to the *identification*, or *call*, number assigned to each book or other cataloged publication. This can be helpful, because it provides a short route to all acquisitions of the library on the research subject without the necessity of inspecting the often-depleted library shelves. Those documents which have not been assigned identification numbers are located through the use of special bibliographies or indexes, which are usually part of the general catalog system; they do not refer to specific items but rather to the general composition of the material. Similarly, those special collections of research material reproduced on microfilm or other miniaturization systems are usually separately cataloged, although reference to the existence of such separate collections and their covering index may appear as one or more cards in the general catalog.

Computerized Bibliographies and Data Banks

In the late 1960s there were very few data banks in the world capable of producing printouts of bibliographical citations. Even these were largely confined to abstracts of literature on the behavioral and social sciences. Today, most of these directories are generally available to researchers with access to remote terminals for the transmission of computerized data.

In general, there are three categories or *systems of information* that can be retrieved from computerized data banks. These are:

1. *Document retrieval systems*, which produce full *texts* of stored documents as computer printouts
2. *Reference retrieval systems*, which produce full bibliographic *citations* for all items or topics classified within a particular subject
3. *Fact retrieval systems*, which produce short, but precise, *answers* to specific questions, mainly within the pure and applied sciences

The main difference between the three information systems is clearly in the nature of the data each includes. Most of the banks currently available to researchers are *reference retrieval systems*, which, in addition to bibliographic citations, can produce abstracts of information if these are requested in the researcher's instructions. Some systems also include complete texts of documents that can be routed directly to the researchers.

In order to utilize data banks for research purposes, the researcher must first decide which of the foregoing systems he wishes to call into action. His decision on this most essential point will be influenced by the considerations discussed in the following subtopics.

The Availability of an Appropriate Data Bank

To make this determination, the researcher should consult either *Fee-Based Information Services* or *Information Industry Market Place*, which provide detailed descriptions of hundreds of organizations in the United States and abroad that produce, process, store, and use bibliographic and non-bibliographic information. Both books are by the staff of R. R. Bowker Company, Ann Arbor, 1981. The first is an entirely new directory while the second has been published annually since 1978 with periodic supplements. *See also* Anthony T. Kruzas and John Schmittroth (Eds.), *Encyclopedia of Information Systems and Services* 4th Edition, Gale Research Co., Detroit, 1981.

Subject Bias of the Inquiry

There is little standardization between data banks on the amount of data they store or how that information is classified for ease of retrieval. To assist in deciding what should be requested, data banks generally provide *descriptors* that detail the exact contents of the data files (tape, discs, etc.). These are helpful in indicating the scope and bias of the computer assisted search.

Costs Involved in Utilizing Data Bank Services

The principal cost factor in a data bank search is the amount of *computer time* involved. This, in turn, depends upon how instructions to the computer are framed. This is facilitated by discussion with the librarian or other technician in charge of the in-house terminal, in order to identify precisely what is wanted and how it can be produced through the data bank system. Most data banks located within academic establishments charge very little beyond the fixed rate, which varies, for computer search time and printout costs. Commercial data banks charge for their services on the basis of computer time, any professional assistance rendered, and sometimes an added *expense factor* that covers miscellaneous out-of-pocket data bank costs.

During recent years, there has been a gradual shift from universities and research libraries that have maintained their own data banks to the utilization of commercial data banks that are linked on a network basis to other data banks in all parts of the country. The result is that libraries and commercial data bank service centers that offer computer *input messages* and *information printout* terminals serve as intermediaries between the researcher and the information storage system at data banks. In this role, the library or commercial terminal center is usually able to assist the researcher by advising on the choice of data files to be searched in order to provide the most efficient and least costly means of locating information on the research subject. The most important part of their help is in the formulation of *precise questions* to be asked the computer in such a way that the maximum information can be drawn from its memory system at minimal cost.

Magazine, Journal, and other Serial Indexes

Magazines, especially, are recognized by researchers as a most important source of information on public management matters. In their recent issues may be found the most up-to-date information on many subjects and events. Events and information of historical interest are usually easily identified through the use of indexes to serials, such as newspapers and periodic trade papers, which date back to the founding of such publications. In addition, there are journals published by specialized technical and trade organizations, as well as publishing companies that devote their entire effort to indexing the articles appearing in these periodicals and serials.

Bibliographies

A bibliography is a *list of writings* on a specific subject. Its usefulness to researchers is second only to the encyclopedias in all but those situations in which encyclopedia articles contain citations to magazines, journals, serial publications, books, and pamphlets. Bibliographies are available for most of the recognized specialties, with most providing coverage on a specialized basis for those disciplines and subdivisions of more current (the past twenty-five years) interest to researchers. Their coverage ranges from brief reading lists, to massive listings of writings on a given subject by a particular author published within specific countries and industries or governments within geographic areas. They serve the twofold purpose of providing information on the content, author, and publisher of specific books and pamphlets and of offering guidance on which books or pamphlets to choose for a given research purpose.

A considerable number of bibliographies have been compiled by special purpose, as well as general libraries. Each month witnesses the appearance of new or revised bibliographies that help in the choice of research material in the book or pamphlet form. Their completion, publication, and availability is usually given news treatment in specialized professional journals and trade papers published on an industry-wide or profession-wide basis.

Newspapers

Because they are frequently the only available sources of information in print on particular events, newspapers should not be underestimated as public management research tools. Newspapers include daily, weekly, bi-weekly, and monthly publications, mainly devoted to reports on current events relating to people, organizations of all kinds, and natural phenomena. Even in situations in which newspapers do not represent the only sources of information, they are important in public management research because they provide a valuable criterion of contemporary viewpoints and a reliable source of data on *when, who* was involved, and *where* the events occurred.

Most of the thousands of newspapers published throughout the world do not have their own indexes, nor are they covered by the newspaper abstracting and indexing services. The exceptions to this, however, cover a fairly wide range of newspapers mainly published in the United States and Great Britain.

Biographies

Searching for information about people, both living and dead, is an interesting aspect of public management research, but a considerable amount of time can be wasted if the researcher does not know where to look. Obituaries, as well as newspaper indexes, often provide guidance to published material on the people who are or have been active in the field of public management. Past editions of *Who's Who* and similar directories are perhaps the most useful biographical resource but do not usually include anyone who has not achieved prominence and do not always provide citations to the works of those they do include.

Government Publications

The governments of the United States and Great Britain not only publish the largest amount of research materials but also cover the widest range of subjects of public management interest. In both cases, cumulative indexes are readily available and should be included in the PMRC's library.

Archives and Manuscript Collections

Archive and manuscript material is useful for researching beyond that that is indexed in bibliographies, etc. It is not, however, as readily available. A great deal of work has been done by archivists and librarians, and this should always be included when tracking down *all that is known* on a particular research subject.

Researchers will find it easier to find and use archival, manuscript, and unpublished material if they have a working knowledge of how archives are developed, arranged, and used. A book by Philip C. Brooks, entitled *Research in Archives: The Use of Unpublished Primary Sources*, fills this need admirably.[1] It is intended primarily for the researcher rather than the professional archivist. It includes an extensive bibliography, is well-organized and exceptionally well-written.

Almanacs

Of the many categories of research resources described in this chapter, almanacs have an information-providing reputation that has lasted since the first was issued in the mid-sixteenth century as a help in predicting good and bad things to come. Today's almanacs still deal with the calendar but have grown in coverage to include a vast amount of carefully checked and edited miscellaneous information in tabular form; narrative articles on events of past and recent popular interest; and comparative information about countries and lesser geographical areas, such as their politics, population, products, cultural trends, colleges, associations, and prominent people.

The researcher will find the *New York Times Encyclopedia Almanac* the most useful and widely imitated. Encyclopedic features, such as a calendar of events a century ago, provision of a list of endangered wildlife species, a dictionary of medical symptoms, and several articles on authors of international prominence, make it a leader among the almanacs available to researchers in most libraries.

---

[1]Brooks, Philip C.: *Research in Archives: The Use of Unpublished Primary Sources.* Chicago, University Press, 1969. *See also* Warnken, Kelly, *The Information Brokers*, R. R. Bowker Co., Ann Arbor, 1981.

Yearbooks

Included in the yearbook category are reviews published either once or twice a year by commercial publishers, but mostly by academic institutions and learned societies as a service to their scholarly readers. Their emphasis is usually on bibliographic references and news on recent research.

Maps and Atlases

While early map collections were often highly inaccurate, they did serve their purpose of providing a fairly realistic picture of the parts of the earth and sky. Today, maps are useful to the researcher because they portray features such as boundaries, transportation routes of all kinds, land elevations, population centers, and temperature zones. They are drawn to accurate scale and frequently supported by tables and comparative graphs, often using color or several kinds of graphic symbols. Helpful explanatory information is usually found at the beginning of atlases or on the cover of collections of separate maps.

Gazetteers and Guidebooks

Gazetteers are *geographical name dictionaries* that are useful to researchers because they contain brief factual information about the places shown on maps. They are most useful when used in connection with maps.

Guidebooks contain research information about routes, transportation facilities, accommodations, and places of scenic, cultural, and historic interest. Travel and guidebooks are useful research tools because they provide geographical information about centers of population and their surrounding areas that helps to portray their individual environment. While they should be capable of standing alone, guidebooks are usually used in connection with atlases and maps. In using guidebooks and maps, the researcher should remember that change is constantly occurring; therefore, it is always wise to note the date of publication.

All countries, usually through their tourism programs, issue guidebooks that are mainly promotional in character, but they often help to identify places, things, and conditions that can be traced further through encyclopedias and technical works specializing in subjects such as geology or agricultural and urban affairs.

Photographic Material Collections

Two research tools deserve mention as much because of their authenticity as *primary research material* as because they have been so underused for governmental research purposes. The first of these is photographic material in the form of black and white and color still photographs and motion picture films. The second is video/audio tapes of events and processes, miniaturized copies of documents (microfilm, etc.), and photocopy exhibits such as slides and overhead projection plates. These latter techniques, mainly resulting from technological advances, have increased photographic capability tremendously. Their importance as primary research sources is vouched because, in many instances, photographic records constitute the prime documentary evidence of what actually occurred.

Since early in the 1950s, serious work has been undertaken to compile photographic records on a wide base, to protect them from destruction from natural and other causes, and to make them accessible to researchers. So far, there has been no comprehensive guide for locating even the best photographic collections, although some archive catalogs refer to their interest in them and list what they have on hand.

Machine-readable Records

The ease with which bibliographic, abstract, and other reference material can be utilized in library research work has already been mentioned in connection with computerized data banks. Closely related to that methodology are records in the form of punched cards, discs, magnetic tape, or some other electronic recording system that are used as computer input media or for making statistical and other types of summaries and analyses. A great amount of information is recorded in this way, used very sparingly for making statistical analyses or summary tabulations, stored for future reference for a time, and then destroyed.

A considerable amount of the data recorded is confidential, and its use is limited by statute in the interest of personal privacy. Much of it is available, however, in summary form that involves no references to individuals. In some cases, individual records can be selected for analysis, but only under conditions in which the identity of the individual is withheld and the agency having the data is satisfied that the request for its use is for an authentic research purpose in the public interest. For example, the United States Census Bureau has files that contain information about *individuals* but will release it only after the data storage equipment has been programmed to suppress responses to requests in geographic units of less than a city block.

RESEARCH-IN-PROGRESS RESOURCES

By the time a researcher has done all he can to explore the information resources described in the preceding subtopics, he will have a good idea of what scholars and fellow researchers have been doing up to, and sometimes including, the recent past. This does not, however, provide a way to avoid the frustration that comes when one completes a project, only to find that someone is planning, has just completed, or is in the process of completing, a project on the same or a closely related subject.

So much is being done in the field of public management that it is virtually impossible to rely on one's own professional contacts or the announcements that pass from person to person in an academic institution, public enterprise, or government agency. There are certain alternatives a researcher can follow to this end.

Professional and Other Relevant Journals

Professional and other relevant periodical publications often carry announcements of doctoral dissertations that have already been filed or subjects that have been approved for dissertation purposes. These also carry articles or pamphlets, announcements, and reviews. All are useful with respect to their contents as well as any bibliographical references cited.

Organization Inquiries

Academic, professional, and trade associations in the public management fields are usually informed on what their members are doing along research lines. They make it a part of their function to keep in touch with trends in their fields of interest, and this means a constant stream of inquiries and follow-up correspondence. These contacts, plus their own research activities, make them a promising source of information on public management research plans, research-in-progress, and completed research that has not yet been published or otherwise disseminated. Also included here are announcements of additions to archives, and other material that may contain useful news that might not otherwise reach the researcher.

Research Center Activity Reports

Announcements of research projects planned, in progress, or completed are often inserted in newsletters, lists of coming events, and annual reports to sponsors. Because their announcements and reports are confined to membership and sponsors (donors especially), the researcher must take the initiative by communicating with known government research centers concerning any activity that may be receiving attention or be planned for the future. All relevant information on such research activities is contained in the *Research Centers Directory*, edited by Dr. Archie M. Palmer.[2]

Charitable and Nonprofit Foundations

Foundation directories provide a short route to information on the funding and/or sponsorship of ongoing research work to which they have previously given financial support. Letters of inquiry based on checking annual reports, and their listing in the

----

[2]Palmer, Archie M.: *Research Centers Directory,* Annually with periodic supplements. Detroit, Gale Research.

Encyclopedia of Associations,[3] should produce names, addresses, and a brief summary of their purposes and programs, including research projects.

PREDICTING SOCIAL TRENDS HAVING PUBLIC MANAGEMENT IMPLICATIONS

The record shows that during the past several thousand years people have persistently and ingeniously sought to forecast future events. For example, the Babylonians developed the pseudo-science of astrology, while numerous other civilizations demonstrated their hunger for foreknowledge in what are presently considered incredible ways. The seeming incredibility of the methods employed has done much to discourage acceptance of recently introduced theories that events and trends can be reliably predicted by scientific methods. To illustrate, the first significant efforts at scientific prediction of social events and trends were the product of the eighteenth century French Enlightenment. An outstanding example of this type of prediction is the *Sketch for a Historical Picture of the Human Mind*, written in 1794 by the Marquis de Condorcet, an encyclopedist and reformer. He predicted many social events and trends that have occurred with a high degree of accuracy and others that, while not yet fully proven, stand an excellent chance of verification in the light of recently developed technology and an accompanying increase in layman, as well as scholarly, interest.

The *Summary of de Condorcet's Social Predictions,*[4] enumerates the seventeen predictions contained in the above cited treatise. In addition to those listed, de Condorcet previously foretold the direction of scientific inquiry in numerous fields, the application of mathematics and statistical methods to the social sciences, and predicted an enormous increase in the volume of scientific research.

The Present Status of Social Trend Prediction

Since the publication of de Condorcet's eighteenth century predictions, numerous less ambitious efforts toward the same ends have been produced in various parts of the world. Notable among them is the 1967 publication of *The Next 500 Years; Scientific Predictions of Major Social Trends*, by Professor Burnham P. Beckwith.[5] Professor Beckwith employs a thoroughly scientific method to deal with prediction durability, rates, and directions. He does this by combining history, logic, and statistical methods in a disciplined and imaginative way to predict *what* will happen, not *how*, and to what *degree* it will happen. In the preface to his book, Professor Beckwith stresses the point that, as a social scientist, he concentrated on social change, leaving forecasts of future inventions and technological advances to natural scientists and engineers. He also makes the point that although the scientific prediction of social trends is both easier and more important than the prediction of inventions, it has received much less attention. This can be attributed to the following:

1. Some social scientists cling to religious and philosophic dogmas concerning freedom of the will that assert or imply that human behavior is unpredictable.
2. Other social scientists believe the causation of social evolution is so complex and so little understood that social events and trends cannot be usefully predicted.
3. Many people who have made plausible, but unpopular predictions, have been denounced or even punished as subversive.

Before discussing the principal methods of management-related social trend prediction, it is well to stress that for centuries most major contemporary social trends have been unpopular, especially outside the scientific community. For example, the movement from farm to urban areas has been going on for the past hundred years in the United States and in Western Europe, despite the popular conception that life is more healthy in a rural environment. Similarly, divorce, family planning, trade unionism, the emancipation of women, free public education and libraries, multiple wage-earning within the family, and greater freedom to emigrate to other countries are among the many examples of social trends that were highly unpopular during the early years of their growth. It follows, therefore, that it is quite probable many of the predictions made on the basis of currently unpopular concepts of needed social change will be

---

[3]Yakes, Nancy and Akey, Denise: *Encyclopedia of Associations,* annual and quarterly supplements. Detroit, Gale Research.

[4]Based mainly on the chronological listing in Beckwith, Burnham P.: *The Next 500 Years: Scientific Predictions of Major Social Trends.* New York, Exposition Press, 1967.

[5]Ibid.

SUMMARY OF DE CONDORCET'S PREDICTIONS

1. The political principles of the French revolution will spread and inspire reform or revolution in many nations.
2. All European colonies in the Americas will become politically independent.
3. European colonies in Africa and Asia will be freed from exploitation.
4. The nations of Europe will increasingly send doctors, teachers, and other experts, instead of adventurers and missionaries, to backward countries.
5. The imminent decadence of the great religions of the East will occur.
6. The laws and customs chiefly responsible for economic and political inequality among men will be radically reformed.
7. Public financial support or social insurance for the needy, especially the aged, widows, and orphans, will be introduced.
8. Education will become public and universal.
9. Scientific research will continue indefinitely to expand human knowledge.
10. More equal opportunities for education will enlarge the scientific community and the scope and number of the sciences.
11. Technology will improve and expand with the sciences.
12. Technological progress in agriculture and industry will support more people on an ever higher standard of living, with less work per person.
13. Women will be given the same legal rights and educational opportunities as men.
14. Wars will be regarded as disasters and become less and less frequent.
15. The progress of the sciences will ensure the progress of the art of education, which in turn will advance that of the sciences.
16. Improvements in medical care, food, housing, labor-saving machinery, and income distribution will lengthen life and improve health.
17. Advances in medical practice will eliminate infectious and hereditary diseases.

similarly slow to gain acceptance, and some may be considered subversive before they are accepted.

This does not mean, however, that education and the evident benefits of many past social changes will not bring about a gradual decrease of opposition to changes now considered subversive by some laymen and experts. Children being raised in a rapidly evolving society are unmistakably demonstrating their capacity for change, and it is probable that some scientific prediction of future social changes will tend to encounter less opposition, a trend that can be expected to continue indefinitely.

Methods of Social Trend Prediction

There are at least seven methods according to which predictions of social change having public management implications can be made. Bear in mind that the concern here is with events and trends, not with precisely *how* they will manifest themselves or precisely *when* they will become effectively accepted. Their inclusion here is to provide the researcher with an overview of an additional research capability. To employ this capability effectively requires substantial historical research, the application of logic, the use of statistical methods, and a very large use of one's own imagination and creativity.

Observation and Investigation of Continuing Trends

There is an abundance of statistical and narrative data on trends relating to sociological developments that may serve as a solid basis for projecting future public management developments, providing there is no observable obstacle or limiting consideration concerning their continuance. For example, long-run trends in the growth of public management knowledge, educational opportunities leading to careers in this field, and the rise in real wages paid for managerial specialists are indicators of future trends.

The principal resources for the prediction of future American trends in most sociological areas are the *Statistical Abstract of the United States*, and *Historical Statistics of the United States: Colonial Times to 1957*, both of which are published by the United States Bureau of the Census and are generally available in public and academic libraries. On an international basis, the *Statistical Yearbook of the United Nations* permits comparisons, as well as trend data that is peculiar to particular nations. Periodical literature, which is usually cumulatively indexed, provides the best insights into current trends with their roots in the past and often provides relevant information on expert views of what trends can be expected in the short- and long-range future, including their public management implications.

Differences between Expert and Lay Opinion

Since the beginning of recorded history, practitioners of management have had ideas about what was best for the present and what might be anticipated in the future. This is not to say that the experts of the time were more or less accurate than the laymen. Thinking about management has been mainly directed toward the development of *methods* to overcome the kinds of barriers encountered in the *past*.

The important consideration here is that lay and expert opinion on *future* program and managerial trends is an indication of the alternative approaches lay and expert opinion considered important *at the time*. It also provides a basis for pinpointing what was happening at any specific time in the management of social programs. For example, at the present time (1981), social reforms separating lay and expert opinion include environmental protection, alternative sources of energy, community health, and the constitutional guarantee of equal rights for women. None of these examples has received either full public or expert approval, but acceptance trends indicate both their eventual adoption, and an extensive incorporation of advanced public management technology in whatever programs emerge concerning each of them.

Inter-governmental Differences

A study of the differences that prevail between governments within a nation as well as those that prevail internationally helps to identify, with a relatively high degree of certainty, what ideas and social programs will prevail in the long-term future. In many situations, the routes that will be followed to reach acceptable goals are unmistakably clear. Since the differences between the *status* of developing public programs tend to be greatest internationally, it is relatively satisfactory to look to the present status of socially desirable programs, such as family planning, preventive medicine, environmental protection, and women's rights, to forecast what should be expected in other locations where these and many other programs have not yet gained a substantial foothold. For example, the differences that have been expressed by experts on the *extension* of specific social insurance programs can be taken as an almost certain sign that acceptance of social insurance reform *generally* will occur in the relatively near future.

Similarly, a study of the differences that prevail between developing countries, as well as those between the more and less developed countries, provides a reliable index to what sociological and therefore public management changes the less developed countries are most apt to adopt. Innovations that appear in one advanced country or region will probably have a better chance of adoption sooner and more extensively in another advanced country or region, than in a less advanced country or region. To illustrate, the United States led the way in developing free secondary and postsecondary education and in the extension of the voting franchise to women. Great Britain pioneered in the industrialization of manufacturing and parliamentary government. France led the world in the adoption of family planning measures. Germany led the way toward an effective large-scale application of compulsory social insurance, while Australia carried out the first experiments with compulsory arbitration of labor disputes. The lesson that researchers in public management can learn from a study of such developments is that when pioneer social reforms prove successful and publically acceptable in developed countries, this is usually a good reason to predict that they will sooner or later be adopted by other *advanced* countries, and increasingly become part of the aspirations of the *less advanced* countries.

Differences in Organization and Program Structure

Studies of the differences that prevail in the organization and behavior patterns between the more and the less efficient public organizations engaged in similar programs can be used as a basis for predicting that the less efficient will gradually adopt the policies and the organization patterns of the more efficient. For example, it is highly probable that medical services will continue to be more extensive and generally better through clinic-type practice as compared with individual medical practice.

Differences in Income Levels

Differences in product and public service consumption habits that occur between the wealthy and the poor of a particular country, region or locality provide the basis for predicting future consumption behavior. As real incomes advance, more and more people can be expected to adopt the consumption habits now peculiar to their more wealthy neighbors. For ex-ample, if there is a gradual rise in *real income* over an extended period of time, it may be safely predicted that activities such as foreign travel, the more extensive use of public libraries and recreation facilities of all kinds, or a close adherence to quick and significant changes in clothing styles will occur more extensively.

Technological Developments

Reports on recent major technological developments, and projections of their social consequences, provide a satisfactory basis for estimating the time and other requirements that will be needed to realize their more extensive application and future development. The researcher in public management techniques will find that records of the introduction of new technology in the past help to predict the directions in which innovative technology will move. Moreover, the inevitable social effects of some major innovations continue for many years, thus making it worthwhile to study the continuing effects of old inventions. For example, the automobile, which was invented over a century ago, will certainly continue to facilitate decentralization of metropolitan communities for at least another century or so, and call for many new and extended public management techniques, such as vehicle storage facilities, mass transit programs and staggered hours of employment.

Science Fiction

The researcher may not find precise descriptions of public management utopias in the writings of modern science fiction authors, but it will not be difficult for him to visualize what techniques are necessary to the solution of logistic problems, such as those relating to an extensive space shuttle program. To illustrate, a researcher in public management need only take a particularly plausible prediction contained in a science fiction novel, and apply one or more of the preceding examples of prediction areas to see whether it can be adequately supported by any of them. While some science fiction contains utterly fantastic and quite unrealistic predictions, many that were regarded as such in the past have become commonplace. Jules Verne's *Nautilus* contained little that a modern nuclear submarine is without, except perhaps an enterprising executive such as Captain Nemo. Irrespective of the often encountered lack of plausibility, the researcher should bear in mind that for a very long time the writers of science fiction were the principal forecasters of future social trends and can still be relied upon to continue the formulation of often brilliant hypotheses.

Chapter 4

THE DATA-GATHERING PROCESS—
FIELD SURVEYS

GOVERNMENTS ARE generally limited in their ability to secure a comprehensive and balanced view of citizen thinking about public management issues. The most usual ways available to them are through personal contacts with individuals and groups, generally in response to complaints, pressures from those with special interests, letters to editors, news columns, editorials, and occasionally through a demonstration with the paraphernalia of slogans, cartoons, and often slanderous accusations. None of these lend themselves to systematic analysis, nor can, therefore, be accepted as the overall view of the people whom the government serves.

Scientifically planned and implemented field surveys offer a means for governments to test public opinion. A field survey, then, represents the best of the various ways to secure citizens' views on matters such as the following:

1. Satisfaction with the level and quality of services received, including the identification of problems and deficiencies
2. The extent of nonuse of public services, including the nature of the dissatisfaction, if any, and what nonpublic services are used instead
3. Potential demands for new or extended services
4. Opinions on community issues, especially those potentially capable of alienating citizen feelings towards the government and its officials

The search for such information stems from the need for it in order to set priorities, to make equitable allocations of funds, to improve existing programs, and to eliminate those which are no longer meeting governmental or public needs.

TACTICAL CONSIDERATIONS IN FIELD SURVEYING

Irrespective of which field survey method is employed, it is important that certain tactical considerations be evaluated, and a determination made on which, if any, of the available methods should be utilized. The following questions under topical headings apply to all four of the methods in varying degrees. For that reason they are summarized here and are augmented later in this chapter only to the extent that their individual importance warrants further discussion.

Assuming that the subject being researched deals with *people*, the following considerations are the most critically important.

Survey Objectives

The first and most important questions that the researcher must ask are what is the purpose of this research effort and what information is needed to fulfill this purpose?

Extent of Coverage

What population group is to be studied? For example, is the study to cover long-term residents as compared with newcomers, or both? Is a particular age group or sex to be surveyed, and why only that population segment?

Nature of Data to be Collected

What steps can be taken in advance to ensure that only *useful* information will be collected? For example, what survey ground rules should be announced in advance, to preclude questions such as should a recent move into the community, a recent change of employment, or the wife's (as a second breadwinner) withdrawal from the labor market be taken into account in questions about sources of family income? Are temporary residents to be included? How are *nonresponses* to be handled?

Data Measurement

Can data collected in previous studies be used for assessing the validity of new data, or in identifying the extent of change that has occurred over a period of time? Should data on health be secured by asking questions or by studying clinical records? If major differences between survey and clinical data are observed, should there be a further effort to determine the validity of the data developed through a survey of the people involved?

Degree of Accuracy Required

Does the use to which the survey data is to be put call for a high degree of accuracy, say less than a 5 percent margin of error? How will that margin be determined? Will a larger margin of error undermine the purposes of the survey to the extent that the credibility of a proposed course of action can be called into question?

Composition of the Survey Sample

Should the survey sample be a neighborhood having generally comparable characteristics (ethnic origin of inhabitants, proportion of youth and retirees, etc.), the city block, or some other geographic unit?

Size of Sample

Bearing in mind that the major political and television program popularity pollsters predict the outcome of elections on the basis of about twelve hundred telephone or face-to-face interviews, what would be a reasonably sufficient number of contacts in the survey to be made? What arguments can be used to support the sufficiency decision?

Data Gathering Methods

What factors prompt a decision in favor of mailed questionnaires, face-to-face interviews, or telephone interviews? Should the interviews be conducted at particular locations, such as schools, other community facilities, or at interviewees' homes? Should only one type of place of interview (school building or supermarket parking lot, for example) be selected, or does this matter? Should professional assistance be secured for the design of questionnaires and the interview structure?

Interview Design

To what extent should interviews be carefully structured and the pattern followed without exception? Should a degree of individual style of *ice breaking* on the part of the interviewers be allowed? Should a mailed questionnaire include assurance that the responses received will be treated with complete anonymity? In this connection, what design considerations should apply to printed questionnaires?

Interview Field Testing

Who is to design, supervise, and evaluate the results of a field test of mailed questionnaires or interviews, and how will any needed corrective action be conducted?

Organization of the Field Team

Assuming that professional interviewers and volunteers (retirees, homemakers, students, etc.) are available, which should be utilized? Is a combination team practicable? If inexperienced interviewers are to be used wholly or in part, what training should be provided and by whom? What supervision will be given as a follow-up to the training and later in the course of making the survey?

Accumulating and Processing Survey Data

Who is to be responsible for enforcing compliance with procedures on how raw survey data is to be summarized and turned in by interviewers?

Data Analysis Procedures

Who is to design the procedure for the coding (or otherwise classifying) of the raw data turned in by interviewers or received in the mail, and who will police conformity with the procedure? Who is to design and supervise the compilation of statistical and other types of summary information produced by the survey team or through the use of questionnaires? Who is to be responsible for developing conclusions, and what information is to be provided to those selected to review and interpret those findings? Are recommendations to be made? Are comparisons to be made, and are specific relationships to be identified and their significance evaluated?

Final Survey Report

Who is to draft the final survey report? What format is to be used? Are working papers, such as interview report summaries and computer printouts, to be provided as an appendix to the report or submitted separately? Who is to receive copies of the report within the organization and/or as interested outsiders? Has agreement upon the matter of confidentiality of findings and recommendations been reached?

Follow-up Action

Would a follow-up, in the form of a subsequent, for example, a year later, review of the use made of the survey findings and recommendations serve to establish the *credibility* of the survey as a research method, and of the organizational element (the PMRC team, for example) responsible for it? If it is found that little or no benefit has accrued from the survey, what action might be taken to correct its deficiencies? What changes should be made in the design and conduct of similar field surveys in the future?

The next four topics are devoted to the most commonly used research survey methods; they are:
1. Face-to-face interviews
2. Telephone interviews
3. Mailed questionnaires
4. Observation of work-in-progress

Guidelines are provided to assist in making field survey decisions and applying proved methodology in their fulfillment.

SURVEYS EMPLOYING FACE-TO-FACE INTERVIEWS

Face-to-face interviews serve a threefold purpose. *First*, discussions, following a question/answer format with someone who has extensive experience of a subject, can help to identify and focus the more important issues or aspects of research problems. The key to success in the use of personal interviews is identification of truly *relevant* information, rather than the historic aspects of the subject. The interviewee's personal judgement on, for example, who did what under past (and different) managements or operating conditions is probably irrelevant under present conditions. The *second* purpose of interviews is to update standard reference books and reports with information about what is happening at the present time. *Third*, interviews reduce the burden of reading reports and other records dealing with past unsuccessful research efforts in the same subject area. It should be remembered that past unsuccessful efforts may not necessarily have been caused by inadequate research. They may have been due to inconclusive interpretation of the data or a lack of interest in the conclusions drawn from it and the recommendations made. Furthermore, by personal interview, it may be found past research assignments were, actually deliberate attempts to sidetrack or delay coming to grips with potentially damaging developments within the organization.

When Face-to-face Interviews are Desirable

Face-to-face interviews have proved especially desirable in the following research situations:

1. The subject matter is unusually complex, in the sense that flat *yes* and *no* responses lack the degree of qualification usually necessary to establish degrees of emphasis, priority, or certainty.
2. The survey seeks attitudes, such as those reflected in unstructured responses in which the interviewee discloses personal opinions, or experiences and repeats views expressed by colleagues.
3. The inquiry is extensive as to depth and range of subject matter.
4. The number of interviewees is, for any reason, limited to a relatively few individuals with special expertise.
5. The inquiry is divided into segments and spread over a period of time, with the same interviewees being called upon at a later date for follow-up information or evaluations of changing situations or opinions.
6. It is possible to secure volunteer interviewers, such as college students, retired persons, civic club members, and friends of the research center, who are willing to devote their time to carrying out its program. Arrangements are sometimes made with colleges to use members of classes (courses) that call for field experience in the application of research methods and for a faculty member to assume responsibility for one or more phases of the research process in which interviewing is the data-gathering method.

Included in the types of research situations in which this method is particularly appropriate are (to cite only three examples):

1. Obtaining authoritative explanations from persons engaged in social, etc., projects and programs.
2. Securing interpretations of the impact of past events from participants or observers of those events
3. Getting assessments of proposed policies, strategies, methods, etc., for use in project planning.

PMRCs are sometimes uncertain whether to conduct surveys through the use of center or research sponsor personnel or to contract with a professional survey firm to carry out the project from inception to final report and the preparation of publicity material. The three principal considerations in reaching a decision on this point are:

1. If the research sponsor intends to use information surveys as the *principal tactic* in carrying out its long-range research program, it will probably be less expensive to develop its own survey staff. If survey work is contemplated on only an occasional basis, however, an experienced survey company would probably produce the best results. The alternative to this arrangement is to assign or employ a well-qualified individual to direct the efforts of the survey team. This alternative has been used effectively in training groups of employees from which a permanent team is to be selected for use in a continuing survey program.
2. To the extent that the PMRC's leadership wants to *promote* the use of field surveys as a research method in overall and departmental program goal-setting and project planning, the establishment of an in-house survey staff helps to underscore the organization's commitment to the idea of progress through research.
3. *Credibility* of findings and recommendations is a vitally important consideration, irrespective of *who* carries out a field survey project. When the subject matter of a survey is politically sensitive, for example, there is always the chance that an in-house survey team will be accused of slanting the conclusions. In such situations, it may be advantageous to employ a respected and entirely independent survey organization instead of using PMRC or research sponsor personnel.

Whatever the reasons for deciding between the establishment of an in-house survey capability or contracting for survey assistance, factors such as personnel regulations, union agreements, etc., must be taken into account because of their impact on the attractiveness of positions in the organization to its professional personnel, as well as to those who might consider transferring to the PMRC in order to engage in survey work.

Whether the survey field work is done with in-house staff, by an outside specialist, or by a combination of these, it is critically important that the officials of the sponsoring organization bear the main responsibility for results. They can neither delegate this responsibility, nor can they avoid making the *basic* decisions on what kind of information is needed, from where it is to come, what degree of completeness and accuracy is acceptable, and to what extent interviews are to be the principal information-gathering method.

Interview Methodology

Interviewing as part of the research methodology must be learned and mastered through practice. While one may be an excellent researcher in other respects, some people lack the kind of personality that invites interviewees to talk candidly on things about which they know a lot. To others, interviewing comes easily and naturally. Whichever type of person the interviewer is, however, he can become a more effective data gatherer by following the next five well-tested and basic rules.

Be Prepared

Being prepared means doing the necessary homework in order to avoid insulting the interviewee by asking questions that could have been satisfactorily answered through advanced preparation. Concentrate instead on filling the gaps in the written record by asking the interviewee why he did things, or decided matters, the way the record shows he did. Be prepared with questions having to do with the interviewee's opinions about things relevant to the research assignment, and his views on the known opinions of others.

Establish Rapport

The success of most interviews depends largely on the interviewee knowing who the interviewer is, what he represents, and the purpose of the interview. Only when he knows these things will he feel relaxed in answering questions or volunteering information about matters he would not ordinarily take the time to tell a virtual stranger. In appropriate circumstances, it will help to establish rapport if the interviewee can be shown why his cooperation will fulfill some personal interest, such as helping to keep a subject about which he has expressed views before the public or helping to gain recognition as an expert for a friend or for himself.

Structure the Interview

During the first several minutes of an interview, controversial matters, or the most sensitive aspects of controversial matters, should be avoided in favor of questions that help to identify precisely the general area of study. Then, when rapport has been established, questions that come to grips with the more sensitive issues can be asked and reasked until a satisfactory response is received or until it becomes clear that further questioning on that aspect of the subject will be useless. If the answers are insufficient, follow-on questions such as "Why?" or "What do you mean?" will often produce a more useful response and even important information that had not been included in the initial question.

Listen

After asking a question or making a statement calling for a response, let the interviewee talk. Interrupt as little as possible except to redirect the interview back to the subject about which information is wanted. It is better, however, to go along with a certain amount of rambling rather than to do too much of the talking.

Record Promptly What was Said

There is no *best way* to record what is said in the course of an interview. Even the best interviewers disagree on how to ensure that they have a record of exactly what was said. Whether longhand, one of the various forms of shorthand, or an electronic recording device is used, it is important to convert the notes or recording to writing while the interview is still fresh in the mind. This allows one to fill any gaps, and make corrections and marginal notes on any body language, especially facial expression changes used by the interviewee, that may give additional insight into what was being expressed in words.

If an electronic recorder is used, the interviewee should always be asked for his permission. If possible, the use of the type of recorder allowing a remotely controlled *pause* or *shut-off* will reduce the amount of transcribing that must be done later. It is often beneficial to eliminate the rambling that would otherwise be recorded. The interviewee should be provided with a transcript of the interview so that he can make corrections or amendments. Unless there is an agreement to use the interviewee's changes, they should be disregarded if they substantially change the original statements.

SURVEYS EMPLOYING TELEPHONE INTERVIEWS

The *difference* between face-to-face and telephone interviewing, apart from the use of a telephone instrument, is the saving of interviewer time, energy, and expense. While it is not always true that telephone interviewing tends to discourage prolonged discussions, this advantage may be offset by missing some related information that would be more likely to come out in a face-to-face situation. Otherwise, the purpose of the telephone interview is generally the same.

The principal advantages of telephone interviews are the following:

1. Travel costs and time are usually reduced, although long-distance telephone costs increase in direct proportion to the time devoted to asking questions and recording answers.
2. If the interviewee is not available, a follow-up call can be made at a different time.
3. Interviewees tend to be a little more willing to be candid in their telephone responses than in face-to-face interviews.
4. The training of interviewers can be continued after classroom instruction and practice calls, by listening in, or recording, trainee telephone conversations.

All that is discussed in the previous topic dealing with face-to-face interviews applies with equal force to telephone interviews. There is one limitation, however, that may restrict the composition of the sample of the population being surveyed. Not everyone has a telephone, nor would those who do not have one be inclined to speak as freely if they were to be called to a neighbor's phone. The implication is that a population sample would be somewhat biased by the exclusion of the most deprived members. It follows, for example, that the telephone interview would not be appropriate for studies of welfare recipients.

Distortions may also arise from situations in which telephone subscribers have unlisted numbers. They are more often the middle-income rather than the lower- or upper-income subscribers. Then, too, some families have multiple listings to cover separately husbands, wives, and children. This may result in a duplication of interviews within the same family structure.

SURVEYS EMPLOYING MAILED QUESTIONNAIRES

The use of mailed questionnaires in public management-related data gathering is perhaps the most controversial, but least expensive of any field survey method in common use. It is sometimes claimed, however, that researchers are biased and that this is reflected in questionnaire design, pretesting, distribution, analysis, interpretation, and in survey conclusions. Nevertheless, it is contended that the reliability of data is more a function of proper research planning than of the method employed in data gathering.

While it is true that data from a questionnaire may not be entirely reliable, the same can be said of data collected by other techniques if improper data collection methods are employed. It follows, therefore, that data may be quite valid when collected by using a properly designed, pretested and conscientiously utilized questionnaire. This observation is borne out by the literature and extensive discussions with pollsters on the subject.

Questionnaire Design and Attitude Measurement by A. N. Oppenheim,[1] provides excellent guidance on the design and use of questionnaires. Because of the complexity of the subject, the following paragraphs are confined to the highlights of questionnaire design, pretesting, distribution, and confidentiality.

Questionnaire Design Considerations

The *Typical Field Survey Questionnaire* provides a proven example of a part of a questionnaire that meets the requirements outlined in this topic. It is illustrated here to demonstrate essential design considerations.

The first and most critical consideration in the design of questionnaires is to *motivate* full, prompt, and honest responses. The ways that have proved most certain of accomplishing this goal follow.

A Letter of Transmittal

This should, like the questionnaire, frankly and honestly tell the potential respondent why the questionnaire is provided, how the data will be used; give assurance that the data will be treated anonymously,

---

[1]Oppenheim, A. N.: *Questionnaire Design and Attitude Measurement.* New York, Basic Books, 1966.

TYPICAL FIELD SURVEY QUESTIONNAIRE [a]

Dear Customer:

We need the benefit of your knowledge to help us to rate local TV repair shops, plumbers, hi-fi repair shops, rug cleaners and other services available in your community.

By combining the experience of many careful shoppers in the Washington D.C. area, personal inspection of facilities, analyses of government records, and other sources, we can identify for you the best service establishments in the Washington D.C. area.

In filling out this questionnaire, simply give us your best judgement on each question. The information you provide will be treated anonymously. To help us process your information quickly and accurately, we ask for the telephone numbers of service establishments. But if you cannot find a telephone number, the name and address of the establishment will do.

We appreciate your sharing your knowledge and experience, and helping us to do the research needed to improve prices and services in our community.

Thank you

(Signature and address of sponsor)

A. TV REPAIR

Please recall the most recent TV repair work you have had done. (If none in the last year or so, please skip to the question on ''Hi-Fi or Stereo Repair'')

What TV repair shop did you use?

Shop's phone number _______________________

Shop's name _______________________

Shop's address _______________________

Please *circle* the number below which best describes how satisfied you were with the shop's performance on each of the criteria listed.

	Very dissatisfied	Dissatisfied	Satisfied	Very satisfied	Cannot rate
1. Fixing TV on first try.	1	2	3	4	0
2. Having TV ready when promised.	1	2	3	4	0
3. Letting you know early how much the work would cost.	1	2	3	4	0
4. Courtesy.	1	2	3	4	0
5. Overall performance.	1	2	3	4	0

Comments _______________________

B. HI-FI OR STEREO REPAIR

Now please recall the most recent hi-fi or stereo repair work you have had done. (If none in the last year or so, please skip to the next question on ''Major Appliance Repair'').

What shop did the work?

Shop's phone number _______________________

Shop's name _______________________

Shop's address _______________________

Please *circle* the number below which best describes how satisfied you were with the shop's performance on each criteria listed.

	Very dissatisfied	Dissatisfied	Satisfied	Very satisfied	Cannot rate
1. Fixing stereo on first try.	1	2	3	4	0
2. Having stereo ready when promised.	1	2	3	4	0
3. Letting you know early how much the work would cost.	1	2	3	4	0
4. Courtesy.	1	2	3	4	0
5. Overall performance.	1	2	3	4	0

Comments _______________________

[a] This sample questionnaire is based on an actual survey of Washington D.C. consumers. It consisted of three additional pages which call for the same information about other appliances and services as well as for information on the respondent's age bracket, education, sex of the head of the household, the type of dwelling, length of residence at the present address, and the number of children between the ages of five and eighteen years.

if that is a relevant factor; and tell why the potential respondent was selected to represent the *community* whose views are respected.

Brevity

Make the questionnaire *as brief as possible*, with the initial questions being easy to answer, the next few being the most comprehensive or difficult, and the last questions gauged to retain the enthusiasm of those who may become bored with the answering exercise.

Personal Questions

If any questions are asked that might be considered personal, resistance can be lessened by providing an opportunity to answer without exact figures regarding age, income, marital status, etc. The response can be made in terms of *categories*. To illustrate, the respondent's age might be indicated by checking a box that provides a two-year spread for the teenage group, a four-year spread for the twenty to forty-year-old group, and a ten-year spread for those over forty. Similarly, incomes can be specified as coming within five thousand dollar spreads instead of asking for exact figures. Those questions which call for answers to personal questionnaires should be at the end of the questionnaire, because they are usually the easiest to answer, and by then the respondent will have concluded whether or not questions that are *too personal* have been asked.

Take a Firm Position

There is a tendency for respondents to follow the course of least resistance, by taking an essentially neutral position when asked to evaluate something by indicating a relative level of performance. Respondents frequently avoid taking a stand by simply choosing the middle ground on a question. To some extent, this can be avoided by giving an *even* number of options from which to choose. This device is used in chapter 8 in connection with the evaluation of researcher performance, where the evaluators are given four options between the highest mark and the lowest on each of several performance qualities.

Closed-End Questions

When questions are asked that call for a straightforward answer, the questions should be phrased as *closed end*. Closed end means the respondent is offered a series of answer options from which to choose the one that *most nearly* reflects his personal opinion or experience. It will simplify the analysis of the data secured through closed-end questions if the respondent is not asked to check more than one option. If there is need for an indication of acceptance with respect to two or more options, the options from which choices are to be made should be listed, each option having its own *degree indicators*. For example, the questionnaire might ask that preferences between acceptable alternatives be numbered in the order of their preference and that *each preference* be assessed progressively on a scale of six *degrees of quality*, ranging from *complete acceptance* to *complete rejection*. The arrangement used in the *Research Performer Evaluation* in chapter 8 can be employed if accompanied by appropriate instructions on the *ordering of preferences* and the *degree of acceptance* of each.

Provide Respondents with a Copy of the Survey Results

Offering respondents a copy of the results of the survey is one way of motivating a full and prompt completion of a questionnaire. If this is offered, it should be a summary of the data and not necessarily contain a complete list of conclusions or their interpretation. It may, however, contain a statement on the adequacy of the responses, information on how the data is being used, and what medium will be employed to disseminate the conclusions reached by the researcher or the organization he represents. Usually a postcard notice to this effect is entirely acceptable.

Utilize the Broadest Practicable Survey Base

Consideration should be given to *demographic questions*, such as age range, sex, geographic location, academic qualifications, seniority, salary range, marital status, etc., because each such factor opens the way to another statistical analysis and possibly to an additional or somewhat broader set of conclusions.

Assess the Value of Each Question

Anticipate what each *piece of information* requested in the questionnaire will contribute to the end product of the research project. If this analysis identifies questions of marginal value to the end result, leave them out because they will call for additional data analysis effort and may introduce negative or difficult-to-explain conclusions. This does not mean that questions should be omitted *only* because they will increase the analysis task or introduce difficult-to-explain conclusions. Each question should have a purpose, and that purpose should be clearly related to a specific and predetermined objective and place in the research report.

Build in Consistency Checks

To the extent possible, a few questions should be widely interspersed in the questionnaire that will check the respondent's consistency. To illustrate, the same question that calls for a *yes* or *no* answer may be asked in two different ways, or two questions that should be answered in the same way might be asked. This technique does not guarantee consistency but clearly demonstrates that consistency is a step towards greater research credibility.

Questionnaire Pretesting

The purpose of pretesting a questionnaire is to find weaknesses that will *prevent respondents from providing needed data* because they do not understand the oral instructions or because the questions are confusing, irrelevant, or cover a range of subjects that seem to have little or no relationship to one another. The methods outlined next have proved successful but do not necessarily represent all that can be done to pretest questionnaires. Other questionnaire design considerations such as the categories of prospective respondents, the subject matter of the research project, and the degree to which respondents are assumed to know about recent developments are also important.

Use a Friendly Group

The best of all ways, including professional help in questionnaire design, to ensure reliability in communicating what is wanted in response to questions of any kind (and this includes interview questions) is to thoroughly pretest each question through the use of a selected group of respondents. A friendly group of acquaintances is preferred, willing to provide prompt and full answers and willing afterwards to participate in an evaluation of the questionnaire based on their personal experience with it. Included here are conferences or conventions held by professional groups having an interest in the subject being researched. The distribution of questionnaires to all participants and an announcement from the floor at a general session have produced a very high level of response almost immediately.

Prepare Instructions and the Transmittal Message Carefully

The most critical consideration in pretesting a questionnaire is the care with which the instructions to the prospective respondents are prepared and communicated. If the instructions appear in a letter of transmittal or on the questionnaire itself or if they are to be supplemented with an oral explanation, care should be taken to ensure that each individual or group of prospective respondents receives exactly the same instructions or interpretation of any printed instructions.

Hold a Presurvey Conference with Respondents

If it is not possible to hold a single meeting for the purpose of going over the questionnaire instructions, an alternative is to hold two or more group conferences.

Make Interview Arrangements

If interviews must be conducted in connection with the use of a questionnaire, care should be taken to arrange for a suitable place, and they should be scheduled so that they limit the number of late arrivers and early leavers.

Make a Preliminary Test Run

If none of the foregoing pretesting approaches is possible, a limited distribution of questionnaires with the transmittal letter, personally or by mail, has most of the advantages of a more personalized test run, inclusive of the distribution that is discussed in the following subtopic.

Selection of Respondents and Questionnaire Distribution

What has been said previously on the use of assemblies of organization members for pretesting a questionnaire applies equally to the selection of prospective respondents on a more random basis and to the distribution of questionnaires to them for completion. It may be possible to gather all that is needed for a research project at one assembly of interested people, such as at an organization conference. Difficulties sometimes arise, however, in securing permission to use meeting time for conditioning those present to cooperate in the interest of a successful research project. The same applies to assembling personal acquaintances for this purpose.

In considering the use of questionnaire distribution methods *other than those employing a captive audience*, the researcher should be aware that a return of over 50 percent is exceptionally good. Returns usually range from 35 percent to 45 percent, and even those are that high mainly because of the experience of the researchers with respect to questionnaire design, letters of transmittal, the selection of distribution media, and who was asked to respond.

If a captive audience arrangement cannot be achieved, more conventional selection of respondents and questionnaire distribution methods must be employed.

Distribution Methods

The first consideration in questionnaire distribution is the *choice of ways to put questionnaires into the hands of prospective respondents*. The use of first-class mail is preferred, and typewritten addressing is preferred to longhand, because it gives a more business-like initial impression so that the enclosure is less apt to be tossed out or put aside for later attention. A good but not too high quality envelope is best, and stamping should be done with actual postage stamps rather than prestamped envelopes or stamping machine imprints. The envelope should have a preprinted return address, preferably that of the institution or organization conducting the research project. The words *Personal and Confidential* should be typed on the envelope. If this is done, the transmittal letter might open with a sentence to the effect that the matter is personal and confidential, in the sense that the addressee's own name and/or position is wanted, and that it will be kept in confidence.

Compilation of a Mailing List

The compilation of a distribution list is nowhere near as difficult as is generally thought. Access to membership lists that cover citizen groups, professional societies, fraternal associations, etc., are often attainable from their secretaries if the purpose of the research is not inconsistent with the organization's goals or otherwise unacceptable. If such lists are used, mention of the source of the list should not be disclosed either in the letter of transmittal or through any subsequent publicity, because members of such organizations frequently contend that their memberships and home addresses are not public property and should be protected accordingly.

Use of Organization Membership Lists

Membership lists become obsolete quite quickly; therefore they should not be used if over three years have elapsed since compilation. If it is a local membership, the addresses may be confirmed through the use of a telephone book or city directory. If this entails too much work, the alternative is to accept the loss of postage, etc., through the relatively small number of pieces that cannot be forwarded. If less than first-class postage is used, there will be no forwarding after the expiration of the addressee's change of address notice to the post office so that there will be no way of knowing how many prospective respondents did not receive a questionnaire and how many did not respond for a reason other than nonreceipt.

Use of a Specialized Who's Who

If a mailing list that is larger than those available in membership directories is desired, inquiry should be made of appropriate associations about the availability of one of the specialized *Who's Who* types of biographical directories. If, for example, the research is on an international scale, *Who's Who* type directories are available in some professional and/or academic fields. As with all such directories, the name and address information may be obsolete, but nondelivery must be considered as part of the cost of using this source of prospective respondents.

Fewer Returns from High Officials

If the questionnaire is intended to reach *high government or corporation officials*, the wastage will be much higher than one directed to less senior and middle-level officials. Those at the highest level seldom see their mail. Those at lower levels are often pleased to be asked their views, providing the burden of a long questionnaire is not overly demanding of their time.

Returns from Acquaintances

The easiest of all prospective respondents to reach are acquaintances. They are usually, however, not in sufficient numbers and are often too diversified to provide the kind and level of coverage wanted so that this selection process must be limited accordingly.

Mailing Criteria

The size of the mailing should depend upon the extent to which the population being surveyed is spread over a wide geographic area, the special interests of the group involved, their status as heads of families, consumers of specific types of services and products, etc. There are no reliable rules that fit all situations. It is worth repeating, however, that the leading commercial pollsters seldom interview or send questionnaires to more than 1,200 individuals.

Use of Follow-up Communications

The number of returns of mailed questionnaires can be increased through intensive efforts, such as follow-up letters, telephone calls, or personal interviews to encourage a response through the use of *persuaders*, such as why the addressee was chosen or the importance of a full response from consumers or other classes of recipients. Such follow-up action may increase returns by as much as 30 percent, but the premailing additional unit cost may run as high as 100 percent or more because of the lesser number of letters.

The Enclosure Method

Mailing costs may be reduced by sending questionnaires with other mailings, such as utility bills, organization announcements and newsletters, or journal inserts. The limitations of this distribution method include reaching individuals whose views are not particularly wanted, and reaching people whose responses might be colored by the other items included in the mailing. It should also be borne in mind that mailing costs are usually relatively minor in comparison with the costs of survey planning, questionnaire design, addressing envelopes, and the accurate enumeration of questionnaire responses. The use of combinations of survey and other mailing material should not, therefore, be assumed to be much of an economy. In any case, it is desirable to interview at least one hundred individuals, personally or by telephone, who have received the questionnaire in company with other material such as that mentioned previously. This sample should disclose whether or not the recipient has been adversely *conditioned* by its inclusion.

Combined Surveys

A final suggestion on survey economy is the possibility of combining surveys so that more than one purpose is served. For example, it may be possible to combine a survey of housing needs with citizen attitudes on the quality and extent of public health, recreation, cultural, etc., services. Financial and manpower participation should be forthcoming through such cooperative arrangements. There is also the possibility of grants-in-aid from other units of government, in situations in which more than one unit of government cooperate in data gathering, each for its own use entirely or for all participating organizations.

For a comprehensive coverage of the techniques and processes of mailing questionnaires, an excellent reference book is Paul Lerdos' and A. J. Morgan's *Professional Mail Surveys.*[2]

Questionnaire Confidentiality

There is no completely satisfactory way to convince prospective respondents that their identity will be concealed. Many prospective respondents refuse to respond for reasons other than fear of disclosure, but those who want assurances are often satisfied by one or a combination of the following:

1. Explain that the entire questionnaire methodology in research is conceived for the convenience of researchers and respondents and that a failure to honor pledges of confidentiality and identity would destroy the employment of the questionnaire method for public management research purposes by others.
2. Arrange facilities in a way that prevents entrance or viewing by others during the course of interviews, preferably, so that interviewees enter and leave by different doors by way of multi-purpose reception areas.

3. Do not *hand* a questionnaire to the prospective respondent. Instead, ask him to take one from a pile consisting of many copies. Similarly, request that completed questionnaires be deposited in a locked box or placed *in*, but not *on*, a pile of completed questionnaires, and announce to the assembly of respondents that none of the questionnaires will be examined until all have been turned in.
4. Do not let respondents identify themselves, and if there is fear that the questionnaire or the seat where it is filled out has been marked in order to identify the respondents secretly, invite those present to change their seats any time they

---

[2]Lerdos, Paul and Morgan, A. J.: *Professional Mail Surveys.* New York, McGraw Hill, 1970.

wish, to trade questionnaires, or select another copy from a common source of supply.

5. If the questionnaires are confined to members of a particular organization or group that has frequent personal contact, inform them that the results of the research will be made available to them.

6. Give assurances that any *open-end questions* calling for an unstructured response or personal assessment will not be published as written but will be paraphrased or summarized, thereby preventing any chance of identification of the respondent. This assurance should be accompanied by positive and actual protection of confidences, by not allowing outside access to the completed questionnaires, and by insisting that others have to be satisfied with as detailed a summary as possible short of actual access to the completed questionnaires.

OBSERVATIONS OF WORK-IN-PROGRESS SURVEYS

The observation of the work-in-progress method of field research usually consists of viewing actual work being done, as well as interviewing in the form of questions asking how, why, when, etc. Included also are the making of time-and-motion observations, methods analysis, analysis of production records, study of performance reports, and an infinite variety of other matters that are best understood by direct, on-the-site observations.

Apart from the interviewing, which is mainly related to getting one's bearings in the work-center environment or on the subject matter, and the types of tasks identified previously, further analysis is not usually within the province of public management research. Rather, it falls in the field of industrial engineering techniques as applied to the study of operations. These are outside the scope of this guide but should not be considered as alien to the work of a PMRC.

FIELD STUDY COSTS

The expense involved in planning and carrying out public management field surveys is the principal deterrent to the employment of this research method. There are many factors that affect cost, some of which cannot be easily anticipated because they are apt to occur as a result of changes in survey plans, population sample refinement or expansion, and the accessibility of particular classifications of persons or organizations. Furthermore, prices change rapidly and tend to vary geographically for the products and services utilized.

The example, entitled *Field Survey Costs*, deals with the costs of the items principally used in field research surveys that employ the use of questionnaires. The data provided in this example is based on a series of surveys that used face-to-face interviews, telephone interviews, and mailed questionnaires. Because the survey teams that reported their cost information kept records differently, it was necessary to adjust certain figures within categories, and to combine others to fit the uniform cost classification system employed in the *Field Survey Costs*. Also, in certain cases, quite minor donations of time, products, and services were made about which no cost record was kept. It is believed the data presented is representative of a great deal of actual experience, although some of it will be out-of-date as prices in general tend to move upward or downward.

The following is a summary of factors that were found to be especially responsible for increasing or decreasing the estimated costs provided in the *Field Survey Costs*.

Consultant's Fee

If a professional consulting firm is employed to assist in the planning and/or direction of the survey, its fee will have to be added. There are no standard fees charged by professional survey firms. Quotations based on individual survey specifications must therefore be used, and added to the typical costs provided in the *Field Survey Costs*. For preliminary planning purposes, it has been found that fees range between forty and sixty dollars per face-to-face interview, and thirty to sixty dollars per completed telephone interview, depending upon the number of questions to be asked, and the distances involved. These fees usually include participation in planning the survey, developing the interview schedule, conducting all initial and field-test interviews, coding the interview information and keypunching the data. They do not usually include analysis of data, or drafting conclusions and recommendations; there-

FIELD SURVEY COSTS*

Cost Classifications	Face-to-face interviews (16 questions)	Telephone interviews (18 questions)	Mailed questionnaires (26 questions)
1. Survey planning and direction	†	†	†
2. Compilation of survey lists	$1,200	$1,100	$960
3. Sample selection, map marking, & staff assignments	420	420	420
4. Interview list preparation & mailing lists	230	215	400
5. Mailing label preparation and checking	0	0	90
6. Questionnaire design and testing	280	280	450
7. Questionnaire duplication, training materials, etc.	945	945	945
8. Questionnaire transmittal letter, return envelope purchase and imprint, etc.	0	0	630 ‡
9. Questionnaire pre-testing	20 @ $240	50 @ $140	100 @ $440
10. Interview and follow-up costs			
• Recruitment of staff	40 @ $380	20 @ $380	0
• Training of staff	2,000	1,000	0
• Interview time including travel, recopying, etc.	9,600	5,300	0
• Telephone calls to nonrespondents to questionnaire to encourage survey participation	0	0	340 @ $2,428
• Follow-up interviews to encourage survey participation	20 @ $240	60 @ $138	0
• Staff supervision	1,300	929	0
11. Travel costs	940	60	60
12. Editing, coding, card punching, listing of data, etc.	1,292	1,187	981
13. Telephone costs	218	3,240	180
14. Postage and mailing service costs	0	0	240
15. Analysis and tabulation of survey data	460	490	480
16. Final report preparation	240	460	350
17. Reproduction and distribution of final report	174	185	196
	20,167	16,469	9,250
Interviewees or questionnaire contacts	1,000	1,000	1,000
Usable interviews or questionnaires	910	848	740
Average cost of usable interviews or questionnaire	$22.16	$19.42	$12.50

---

*All data adjusted to reflect estimated costs on the basis of a research survey of 1,000 face-to-face interviews, telephone interviews or mailed questionnaires. Data was collected in 1976 and is subject to an upward adjustment of approximately 4% per annum thereafter.

†Survey planning and overall direction costs are assumed to be borne by the sponsoring organization such as a government agency, business department or a research center. If otherwise, the cost of this classification of expense must be correspondingly increased.

‡Transmittal letter may be incorporated in the questionnaire as illustrated in the Typical Field Survey Questionnaire. If a mailing service is used, add the cost of this often volunteer service. If the questionnaires are mailed with other material, such as utility bills, reports, etc., an appropriate deduction may be made.

fore, particular care should be taken to make sure this service is, or is not, included in the consultant's quotation.

Cost Increase and Decrease Factors

Cost Increases

The most obvious way to increase costs is to employ interviewers who are highly qualified by knowledge and experience. Another is to increase the number of persons, businesses, or households covered. Beyond these cost increase factors, the number of questions included in the survey, the precision with which the survey group is selected, the geographic distance that interviewers must telephone or travel, and the extent of training given to interviewers are all subject to decision in advance of launching the survey.

Cost Savings

Cost savings can be made with respect to all of the previous factors by looking for bargains and by accepting donations in the form of cash, materials, or services. In addition, cooperative or time and materials donation arrangements with other organizations, such as colleges, service clubs, other research centers, trade unions, and consumer groups, can reduce the work and, therefore, the cost of developing interview lists, preparing training and procedure/ policy manuals for the use of interviewers, and programmer and computer time.

Financial Records

If organization personnel are used and paid through departmental budgets, a precise record of the cost of their services should be included in any financial statement issued on survey costs.

Cooperative Mailing of Questionnaires

If the mailing of questionnaires is part of the mailing of other material, such as utility bills, organization announcements, journals, newsletters, and annual and other types of organization reports, the cost of postage and mailing service will be reduced accordingly.

Follow-up Communications

If follow-up mailings or phone calls are made to those who do not return questionnaires, this cost should be included in both the count of contacts made, and the cost of follow-up interviewing by telephone or face-to-face interviews.

Chapter 5

THE DATA-GATHERING PROCESS— ORGANIZATION STUDIES

STRICTLY SPEAKING, there are as many different organizations as there are organization managers, and for this reason, the Public Management Researcher (PMR) needs a wide experience of different types, in order to acquire ideas, such as those discussed in this chapter, that can help him/her to analyze organizations in an effort to detect why they are unable to fulfill their public service mission. However many guidelines are suggested for reference purposes, the PMR must always bear in mind that organization is an *evolutionary process*. The rules that apply today may be the fallacies of the future. Organizations, especially government organizations, are constantly adjusting to new situations. They are dynamic and must be alive to needs that result in growth and development. They respond to lessons that their own experience and the experience of other organizations demonstrate. The capacity to change is essential if an organization is to survive, but at the same time, there is a latent countermovement that seeks stability and consistency and resists efforts to change. The conflict between need for adaptation and resistance to change is fraught with pitfalls because organizations must keep abreast of developments occurring in all the areas in which they exist, or they will collapse for want of ability to deal with the problems for which they have been created.

THE SCOPE OF ORGANIZATION STUDIES

A knowledge of organization theory and practice is also essential to the PMR. Such knowledge is particularly important for those working in government, where the size, complexity, and ever new and increasing responsibilities of government organizations demand carefully planned, simple, and understandable organization structures.

Usually early in his career, the PMR will find himself a member of a team responsible for studying organization structures or for documenting an organization that has already been approved. A basic knowledge of organization is also required if the PMR is to do meaningful work in the methods and procedures field, where organizational relationships and responsibilities are critically important. There are probably very few assignments in public management research in which a general knowledge of organization will not be of great value.

Organization Study Terminology

The PMR should possess a clear understanding of the vocabulary used in organization study. Unless these terms are completely understood, much of what follows in organization study will be meaningless.

Line Organizations

Line organizations are units of government organization performing the basic functions for which the agency was created. In a state or county department of agriculture, for example, the extension agents carrying out field training and demonstration activities would be performing *line* functions.

Staff Organizations

Staff organizations are units of government organization that support, serve, or audit the line functions. Typical staff or service activities are personnel, purchasing, statistics, planning, and accounting, all of which exist primarily to service, advise, or exert certain types of control over the basic line functions.

Support Services

Support services are sometimes considered staff services, but this term tends to confuse, rather than identify, the scope of the services performed and for whom they are performed. For the purpose of this chapter, support services are those day-to-day services that are intended to relieve professional, and other highly specialized personnel, of the burden of doing for themselves those things that could be done by lower paid and lower qualified clerical, technical, custodial, and messenger personnel.

Responsibility

Responsibility may be defined as the obligation of those assigned various duties, functions, and activities. Examples would be responsibility for assessing and collecting taxes, storing and distributing flour, preparing employee payrolls to meet established deadlines, or supervising a clinic in a health center.

Authority

Authority is the power assigned to a position or an individual to give orders and require obedience. It is useless to give responsibility for an activity if authority to do what has to be done to carry out that activity is not also given. The responsibility for operating a government warehouse, for example, means little if the employee in charge does not have the authority to implement the mechanics of operating the warehouse, such as disciplining employees or ordering maintenance of and repairs to the building.

Accountability

Accountability means being held answerable for actions taken and decisions made. It is inseparable from authority. It is not enough for authority to be given; there must be a *holding to account* by a superior, to determine how the authority was used by a subordinate.

Function

Function is a major identifiable part of a total organization effort, as opposed to an *activity* that is usually a portion of a function. Examples of functions are the following: training, personnel management, cost accounting, engineering, and purchasing.

Centralization

Centralization refers to the retention of control of certain functions, actions, or decisions at relatively high levels in the organization. An organization in which most actions are referred to top management for decision would be called highly centralized. Centralization, therefore, must be discussed in terms of *degree*. It may also have geographic meaning in organizations that conduct their activities over large areas. For example, in a highway department that has personnel working in all areas of the county, centralization may well mean physically locating the department's vehicle repair activities in a central garage.

Decentralization

Decentralization means the assignment of decision making to the lowest *practicable* levels in the organization. A highly decentralized organization might have divisions that have almost complete authority for establishing budgets, procuring facilities and supplies, hiring and firing personnel, determining capital improvements, and program planning. Centralization and decentralization can exist side by side in an organization. Operating authority may be highly decentralized, for example, while capital budget approval may be centralized.

Communication

Communication is a word used to describe how units in an organization *talk* with one another. *Downward* communication describes how top management gets its ideas, policies, and directives down into the organization for action. *Upward* communication may be used to describe how lower levels of management report results, trends, and attitudes to top management. Communication *across* is a term sometimes used to describe how one organization unit, such as personnel, talks with another, such as finance.

CONVENTIONS OF ORGANIZATION DESIGN

An organization must always be viewed as a means of getting something done. It is never an end in itself. Almost anyone, after some study of various types of organizations, can sit down and draw an organization structure that closely follows known principles, but the competent PMR develops a graphic representation of an organization structure only after a detailed analysis of its applicability to, and workability in, the function that he is studying. He usually looks at organization structures as a number of *boxes* of authority, responsibility, and accountability that are connected by communication lines representing the flow of policy, planning, direction, control, and co-ordination.

An organization network exists primarily to assist administration to get its policy and program directives down to the *doing* elements of the organization as quickly and as accurately as possible and to ensure that top management gets back, as quickly and accurately as possible, a picture of how the organization is meeting its goals so that any needed corrective action can be taken. It is against this concept of the flow of directives down and the counterflow of information up that the principles of organization are discussed in the paragraphs that follow.

Organization Missions and Objectives

It may seem an obvious step, but often no written statement is developed that communicates to others the mission, objectives, and policies of the organization. Legislation may establish the basic objectives, but policy and goals still have to be developed. They are an indispensable guide to both long-range planning and day-to-day operations. For the organization planner, they are essential in determining responsibilities, reporting relationships, and determining the type and size of organization structures required now and in the future. When no statement of mission and objective exists, the PMR is without the basis on which to structure and report his/her study findings.

Mission Characteristics Should Determine Organization Structure

The PMR should start the organization study by asking himself, *what was the agency created to do?* He/she should be concerned with describing the organization in terms of its basic functions rather than around people. This is illustrated with the following series of conceptual guidelines.

An Organization Plan Should be Simple and Economical

Every effort should be made to keep the number of organization units and management levels at an absolute minimum. Every unnecessary unit and level not only adds to the cost of the operation but makes coordination more difficult and greatly increases problems of communication. This is particularly true in agencies of government carrying on programs on a national or statewide basis, where excessive levels of managerial authority prevent quick decision making and often cause confusion in direction and control. The PMR should be able to identify and explain the justification for each level of supervision. There is a natural tendency for operating officials to build *deep step* organizations that interpose too many levels of supervisory responsibility between the manager and the people actually doing the work. In this arrangement, the manager will sometimes find it difficult to get policy directives down through each successive layer and still more difficult to get reliable and *unscreened* information back up through these levels. A *shallow* organization plan is, in general, more effective, because there is a more responsive delegation of authority in a downward direction to the points at which action occurs. More is said about the documentation (charting) of organization structure in a subsequent subtopic.

Decision Centralization at the Top Level of Management

The answer to the question of *how* and *to what extent* activities of the organization are to be centralized or decentralized is often left to chance or relates mainly to the individual abilities of key supervisors. Centralization/decentralization decisions should be made consciously and with purpose. Certain decisions must be centralized at key points in the organization in order to do the following:
1. Establish objectives
2. Determine policies
3. Provide leadership
4. Establish direction
5. Facilitate meaningful control

Centralization, however, does not mean centralization of routine operational decision making. All too often no distinction is made between *policy making and direction* and *routine operation* with the result that every decision tends to be referred to the policy level, regardless of its importance, or the reverse, in which top level decisions are made by low level operating personnel. The challenge to the PMR is to make clear the distinction of policy versus operation and recognize that responsibility, authority, and accountability should be decentralized to permit operational decisions as close to the point of action as possible. Such decentralization at the working level is most important in large government agencies or public corporations, where failure to decentralize working decisions often results in headquarters units being overloaded with routine, making decisions when they are not informed on the facts, and failing to do their more important planning and control work.

Decentralization and centralization are very relative terms. There is not, and cannot be, anything absolute about either of them, because they are more in the nature of a continuing process than of a static state of organization. This is because there are always competing forces at work in both directions. It is relevant, therefore, to summarize here the most important forces that influence the more desirable movement toward decentralization. Those which have been found most significant are the following:

1. Certain management powers are and should be *reserved* from the outset and not delegated. These include the area of program planning in the organization-wide sense, coordination of interagency effort on a government-wide basis, and evaluating programs within the same ranges.

2. Authority and responsibility cannot be effectively delegated until *policies have been decided* and sufficiently spelled out in an official form capable of uniform administration. Even when this is not feasible, it may be more desirable in the interests of efficiency, economy, and consistency to keep them centralized.

3. Activities that are carried out over a *wide geographic area* are generally the most practicable ones to decentralize. This is especially true if the program involved is one that calls for a relatively large and frequently needed number of on-the-spot decisions.

4. There are apt to be situations with *potentially important implications* that under normal circumstances would not call for central government participation. In anticipation of such unusual situations, it may be desirable to identify specifically those limiting provisions to delegations of authority and responsibility to decentralized agencies. In such cases, exposure to criticism, if matters are mishandled, is usually the unstated reason for making what appear to be inconsistent withholdings of authority.

Lines of Authority and Accountability

As much as possible, an organization plan should reflect at all levels an approved and clear line of responsibility, authority, and accountability. The accountability of a position for the actions of subordinates must be as clear, specific, and absolute as practicable so that responsibility both for successes and failures can be pinpointed quickly and appropriate action taken promptly.

To the extent that specific assignments of responsibility *can* be made, they *should* be. It follows that, to the extent they are made, they should be done with a view to establishing authority to carry out the mission of the government in whichever area of activity is concerned. Nevertheless, while the assignment of each function to an agency may be desirable and, indeed, may help to ensure specific performance, it does not always follow that effective results are prevented if assignments are made with *shared* authority. The PMR must be alert, therefore, to the possibility of strengthening government programs by designing ways for instituting cooperative undertakings. He must also demonstrate how they will be strengthened and made more viable by joint participation. The following observations illustrate this point more specifically:

1. *Organization* means division of work in any one of several ways. This implies a common responsibility for the end result of all work done toward the accomplishment of the organization's mission.

2. *Planning* is a joint responsibility that is shared by representatives of all phases of an agency's program. A weak link in the planning process results not in a plan, but merely in a set of *hopes* that have only a limited chance of realization because of the limitation that results from that weak link.

3. *Public goodwill* depends not on the actions of one public agency, but rather on the overall impression created by all agencies of a government rendering services and enforcing laws.

4. *Certain staff agencies* are created for the purpose of developing policies, planning ways of accomplishing desired results, rendering highly technical services to the line departments, and representing the head of the organization in areas in which he/she has neither the time nor the knowledge to meet the need for enlightened leadership. In such cases, the conduct of effective programs is most often the result of joint effort in developing the services involved.

While there are abundant opportunities for interorganization cooperation and it may not always be desirable to identify specific assignments of authority, it should be emphasized here that if such a delegation is made, then it should be clear-cut and so specific that there will be a minimum of confusion as to who is actually to be held accountable for what.

The foregoing considerations lead to the observation that authority is shared more often than it is totally assigned. This observation leads to another; the word *authority* has various meanings that tend to become confused and call for such clear-cut guidelines in the hands of the MSR who must always make his findings understood as follow:

1. Authority may mean the formal *power* that is legally delegated to an official, to act on behalf of the organization he represents, to issue orders and take the necessary steps to secure enforcement.
2. Authority may mean that the official concerned has the *option* of accepting or rejecting instructions from other sources, in relation to the work of his area of assigned accountability.
3. Authority may mean the power *inherent* in his position, just as a supervising fireman has the power to enter burning buildings to eliminate the hazard of a widespread conflagration.
4. Authority may mean having extensive *knowledge* of, or possessing strong convictions regarding, a subject.

In discussing present organizational arrangements or proposed organizational adjustments, it should be made clear to those concerned, that the PMR is principally concerned with the *first* of the four described uses of authority.

Duplicating and Overlapping Functions

Discussion surrounding the organization principle that unnecessary duplication and overlapping of functions should be avoided contains the word *unnecessary*. Rather than labor this discussion with an attempt to draw specific lines between necessary versus unnecessary, a more useful result will be achieved by accepting the contention that unnecessary duplications of effort tend to be wasteful, but that there are circumstances in which duplications should be encouraged. In some circumstances, not to duplicate would be most wasteful. The following are such cases and should be taken into consideration by the MSR in discussing his findings:

1. Certain functions, such as filing, keeping attendance records, and mounting guards to protect persons and property, can be duplications *without doing the same work.*
2. Vertical duplication is involved to a certain extent whenever the work of an employee is subject to some supervision from above. While

an additional level of knowledge is usually applied by the supervisor, he/she cannot and should not be *selective* in what he reviews of his subordinate's work. To the extent that he/she applies his/her knowledge to those things to which his/her subordinate has already applied his/her knowledge, there is a duplication, but not necessarily a wasteful duplication.

3. Staff and line organization units almost always function in the same fields in areas such as staffing, budgeting, product usage analysis, and the like. This is not duplication because the point of view of the line and staff is different, and because they each seek related, but different, goals, usually by different routes.
4. Occasionally, duplication is desirable in connection with a planned effort to bring maximum force to bear on a problem. In operations research, for example, there is a deliberate bringing together of different points of view (mathematics, physics, personnel, management, etc.) in order to achieve a *cross-fertilization of thinking.* A similar situation occurs when two or more persons interview a candidate for a position.

Channels of Communication and Control

The organization structure is a network that provides for orderly communication and control over activities. The solution of the communication problem—*who talks to whom*—while difficult, can be resolved with continued managerial supervision. Managerial control requires preplanning of performance goals and setting the criteria according to which performance will later be evaluated.

The problem is that the bigger and more complex the organization, the more difficult it becomes for the PMR to see what is really happening. A common device for *seeing* is a formalized system of organization, reporting on results and communicating changes.

An organization, therefore, should permit ready conversion of masses of operating data into control information at significant points in the organization. The head of a medical department, for example, must regularly review summarized data of thousands of clinic visits, hospital admittances, disease rates, birth statistics, and accident information, in order to take action to prevent or cope with possible epidemics, and provide necessary care, as well as to plan his long-range program of preventive medicine and hospital construction. Unless there is a logical and clearly understood manner of reporting such information, control becomes virtually impossible throughout an organization network.

Span of Control

The *number* of positions reporting to *one supervisor* is called *span of control*. This concept holds that there is a limit to the number of positions that an official can effectively supervise. The PMR will find, however, that this number is not fixed, but varies from situation to situation depending on the nature of the work. Thus, a supervisor of a typing pool could be expected to supervise effectively many more typists, than the head of a scientific research laboratory could effectively supervise research workers. The differentiating factor in this case is that the work of the typing pool is highly routine, mechanical in structure, and demands a minimum of individual supervision. Scientific research work, however, is often a team effort of a largely nonroutine nature requiring a maximum of coordination. *Too many* subordinate positions limit the superior's ability to plan, direct, and control. *Too few* subordinate positions usually result in oversupervision and wasted effort. A one-over-one, or one-over-two, situation, for example, is not usually justified. It is usually possible in such cases to eliminate completely the middle layer, with the result that there is often an opportunity for saving lower level positions, and sometimes additionally an existing layer of supervision.

In general, the foregoing statement should be considered a guiding policy, but, like most other conventions discussed in this chapter, it is invariably subject to modification in specific situations. There are at least three such situations in which the idea breaks down completely, and properly so, as follows:

1. The *assistant to* and *deputy* concepts are both predicated on the idea of two officials sharing the authority inherent in the senior of the two positions. When this is properly carried out, all subordinates in the chain of command are automatically accountable to two supervisors.

2. All staff units of an organization theoretically act in the name of the chief executive official, as specialized arms for the development and enforcement of his policies. In carrying out their mission, they are issuing directives or exercising control over subordinates who do not report to them at all.

3. Officials who are endowed with dynamic personalities or who are especially well-qualified with knowledge and experience, frequently achieve positions of informal leadership that result in their exercising actual control and on some matters they may be obeyed as though they had actually been assigned decision-making authority.

Among the factors that have been found most influential in determining the optimum span of control in actual practice are the following:

1. If the routines being followed are simple, substantial in volume, and repetitive, large numbers of personnel are easy to supervise. If the opposite work characteristics exist, only a small number of employees can be effectively supervised.

2. Physical proximity to the supervisor generally calls for the same considerations as work characteristics, such as volume fluctuations, concern with static versus dynamic activities, and the degree to which policy-making decision authority has been delegated downward to the supervisor and from him to at least one lower level of operations. The critical factors here are the degree of reliance that can be placed upon the supervisor and how far he/she can rely upon his subordinates to maintain a high standard of performance through the exercise of *self-control*.

3. The reliance that the organization units must place upon staff specialists for guidance can produce a potentially dangerous supervisory situation. If the reliance is heavy, the span of control should be small, in order to prevent a de facto shift of responsibility from the supervisor to the staff technicians.

4. In situations in which there is an interaction between subunits within an organization, the need for direct supervision becomes increasingly necessary to the coordination of effort. The need for supervision should be measured against the degree of subunit interaction and then adjusted to meet changing needs for additional or lesser amounts and kinds of supervision.

5. It is frequently necessary for a supervisor to devote a large part of his time to interagency relations, thus absenting himself from his duty station. In such situations, consideration of a redefinition of duties should occur before introducing other organizational adjustments. Only in rare instances can an organization be left to run itself while its head is absent for prolonged and frequent periods. A plan for compensating for absences by subdelegations of authority may therefore be appropriate.

6. Depending upon the level of supervision in

question, duties are often performed that are auxiliary to day-to-day requirements. Additional responsibilities, such as participation in agency-wide planning, program evaluations, staff productivity reviews, and the like, all tend to enhance a supervisor's value as a supervisor so that any limitations that are put in the way of such participation should be removed as fully as possible through devices that spread supervisory duties over a broader base within the organization structure.

Coordination Between Positions

An organization must set limits on who may officially contact or communicate with others and how they are allowed to communicate. A local agricultural extension agent, for example, should not be permitted to bypass his/her local district director of agriculture and communicate with a headquarter's extension group on policy matters. Such a practice would invariably create confusion.

This does not mean, however, that all contacts must go through channels. There may be many instances in which information of a routine nature may be required. It would be wasting the department head's time and cause unnecessary delays to go through the formal chain of command in such cases. In order that the manager may exercise his coordination responsibility effectively in every case in which activity bypasses his/her superior, the head of the unit should nevertheless keep his/her superior informed of the following:

1. Any matter for which the superior may be held personally accountable
2. Any matter of disagreement or decisions that are likely to cause controversy
3. Any matter requiring the advice of the superior or his/her coordination with other organizations
4. Any matter involving recommendations or discussions of changes in established policies or practices

To summarize, it is failure to keep superiors informed of actions that usually causes problems in control, communications, and working relationships. Comparatively, this is more important than actual bypassing. Insistence on always following the organization structure or on going through channels when making contacts can result in great rigidity and loss of time. Failure to set some controls on contacts however, can only lead to confusion and loss of control.

Decision Making in the Hands of a Few Responsible Officials

An organization plan should place overall responsibility for making decisions in the hands of specific line executives. While this organization convention seems simple, there is often a tendency to attempt to place committees of staff executives in decision-making roles. Committees should never be allowed to become decision-making groups. Committees can be useful for obtaining different points of view, giving counsel, and functioning in an advisory role. A so-called decision-making committee all too often fails because there is no one person who feels responsible for carrying out the decision, nor is there one person who can be held accountable for the decision. Staff groups should only be established to plan, counsel, advise, and audit. They should report to line decision makers but should not themselves be decision makers.

Flexibility in Organizational Planning

The PMR should always obtain sufficient background data so that he/she is aware of future contractions or expansions of the organization that he/she is studying. Any organization proposals that he/she is called upon to report should provide for such changes so that major reorganizations will not be required as workloads change.

There appears to be a consensus among those who have studied organizations extensively that the more they observe, the more they appreciate and respect their dynamics, inconsistencies, variety, and paradoxes. These can be quite legitimately compared to war because both are characterized by their essential disorderliness. Probabilities, rather than certainties, play the dominant roles.

It can readily be seen in what has been said in the preceding paragraphs that generalizations about organization are loaded with qualifications, warnings about the limitations of *rules*, and exceptions encountered in the attempt to apply preconceived *principles* of organization. The best organizations will continue to be the result of intelligent application of insight and research methods with heavy loadings of intuition, inspiration, ingenuity, experimentation, and a lot of lucky breaks in the form of governmental agency willingness to tolerate trials and errors at the hands of PMRs, and those organizations which utilize their fact-finding and synthesizing expertise.

LINE AND STAFF ORGANIZATION RELATIONSHIPS

It has already been shown how the growth of an organization forces the manager to look for specialized assistance. He/she needs legal guidance, purchasing advice, assistance with personnel matters, and financial planning—all specialized subjects requiring highly trained individuals. These staff specialists must also exert their influence to see that their activities are carried out in accordance with agreed standards, policies, and procedures. How to accomplish this task without actually interfering with lower level line supervisors, who are responsible for end results, sometimes becomes a difficult problem. It is a problem that cannot be solved completely by written rules and procedures, but rather through understanding and appreciation by the staff person and the line person of each other's functions. These relationships will usually work smoothly. Where disagreements arise between officials at the same, or approximately the same, level of authority (with respect to their own area of operation) that cannot be reconciled by discussion, then the logical course of action is to call upon the next higher level of authority to which the disagreeing officials both report.

Observation of numerous line and staff relationships shows that the line manager has a number of complaints against the staff manager. The PMR should be alert to the existence of the following contentions:

1. Staff people try to take over line responsibility by giving orders without reference to line managers.
2. Staff often give poor advice because they don't take the time to get to know operating conditions, nor do they check their conclusions carefully with those who will have to carry them out.
3. Staff do not keep the line informed. For example, a staff person may undertake important studies or participate in discussions that may result in important changes in operations and policy. In too many cases, the first time the line manager hears of the change is the circular or regulation putting the new plan or policy into operation.
4. Staff tend to take a narrow view of problems. Personnel or accounting people, for example, often see everything in terms of personnel or accounting and fail to appreciate important overall operational problems that confront the line.

The staff people have complaints against the line executives as follow:

1. The line do not know how or when to use staff. In some cases, the line do not even know that there are specialists to whom he/she can turn in solving certain problems. He/she is not aware that the problem that appears unique to him/her may have been faced several times before by the staff specialist. In many cases, the line manager lets a given problem go too far before turning to the staff for help.
2. The line resist new ideas. The frequent reaction of a line official to a new idea is negative, even before he/she has weighed its merits.
3. The line often do not give the staff worker enough responsibility. The line do not turn to him/her often enough, state their problems, and ask him/her to present ideas and recommendations. The line do not consider the staff a partner in the solution of important problems.

A SYSTEMS APPROACH TO ORGANIZATION STUDY

The PMR's first organization analysis challenge is to find out why the organization he/she is studying is not reacting to the need for change. Each of the following areas of analysis, expressed here as questions, should have the fullest attention. These questions should not, however, be considered all-inclusive, but rather as providing a summary of workable guidelines within a research framework.

How has Authority been Distributed?

A faulty delegation of authority to make decisions and take action may be the cause of the inability to respond to the need for change. The ramifications of this situation are too numerous to discuss here, but it should be noted that when the more obvious *formal* deficiencies of an organization have been identified, there is still the *informal* organizational structure, where the interplay of organizational forces is capable of preventing change by the most subtle of pressures. An organization that has delegation of authority deficiencies can best be strengthened by the following:

1. Establishing new or additional centers of authority, capable of countering reluctance to change by being made responsible for introducing new ideas, such as budgeting, long-range planning, and the like

2. Introducing a greater degree of specialization, which will usually lead to a diversification of authority
3. Establishing profession and/or employee development programs, through which new ideas will be communicated and tested on an experimental basis

How Does the Formal and Informal Communication System of the Organization Work?

If the communication links between the horizontal and vertical elements of the organization are not functioning effectively, the entire system will suffer from lack of viability. The two main deficiencies in an organizational communication system are usually in the areas of *congestion* and *distortion*; therefore, corrective action must consist of an attack on the communication techniques employed. This is in order that communications of all kinds may be speeded up in areas where

1. Speed is important, and
2. Indoctrination is made more precise and selective, so that opportunities for misunderstanding are reduced to a minimum.

The *content* of internal communications is often far more important than the *speed* with which they move from the point of origin to the personnel directly concerned. This is known as *performance feedback*. For example, employees should be informed of exactly what performance is *expected* of them prior to their undertaking work assignments, and this should be followed with regular and frequent *assessments* of how well they have performed according to the standards established for the various categories of work.

Is Low Employee Morale Preventing Organizational Effectiveness?

The causes of low organizational morale are certainly among the most difficult of organizational characteristics to identify and correct. The symptoms are intangible, but nevertheless important to healthy organizational growth and acceptance of change.

The principal symptoms of emotional *health* in an organization are as follows:

1. A prevailing feeling of self-sufficiency, security, and confidence in the rightness of current efforts
2. Optimism and a generally creative approach in a continuing search for more and better answers to current operational problems

In contrast, the symptoms of *low organizational morale* include an atmosphere of fear, insecurity, disintegration, and preoccupation with building defenses and counteroffensives against criticism.

These symptoms tend to reflect the personal attitudes of one or a few individuals who occupy positions of power; however, it is not only the attitudes revealed by people in positions of authority that influence organizational morale. There may also be a pattern of employee recruitment in which doubtful values such as conformity and adaptability are rated excessively high in the appraisal of a candidate's potential.

Corrective action must be kept in the hands of the appropriate officials of the organization under study. The PMR can, however, report suggestions based on his/her observations. When situations such as those described previously are disclosed in the course of an organizational study, suggestions for corrective action (if called for in the T/R) will usually focus on the following areas:

1. Redefinition of the responsibilities carried by the most senior of the supervisors
2. Rearrangement of the physical set-up to create small specialized groups, within which incentives and other morale-building devices can become more meaningful
3. Rotation of routine work assignments to give relief from the more monotonous tasks
4. Requiring each supervisor or the senior official of the organization to train an understudy to be deputized during his/her absence

Is Creative Capability Ignored or Used Inappropriately?

Ignoring or inappropriately using creative capability as an organizational characteristic needs to be appraised, because it is a definite indication of a lack of organizational *maturity*. To identify it usually requires a meticulous study of the processes followed in the areas of recruitment, selection, and training methods with respect to the following:

1. Indoctrination and orientation of new employees
2. Upgrading of the knowledge and skill of employees who are at mid-career through training programs
3. Executive or professional development of those who have too little time at their disposal to devote to fundamentals but need to be kept

abreast of new public administration techniques

Most important to the utilization of employee creative capability are executive attitudes that support experimentation, service improvement suggestions, increasing operational efficiency through adoption of new ideas, and the like.

Are Personnel Being Properly Utilized?

To secure a satisfactory insight into how personnel are being utilized and, also, to provide a useful analysis tool for the PMR that will demonstrate operational findings, two closely related charts should be prepared.

The Task List

A *Task List* is at once the first in a series of closely related research tools and at the same time one of the few source documents that provides the PMR with information essential to any appraisal of present operating procedures and methods. A Task List is a printed form on which each participant in an activity records the tasks he/she performs during the course of the day, week, or month and indicates how much time he/she devotes to each task.

GUIDE TO TASK LIST PREPARATION. It is essential to explain fully the purpose of Task List preparation to employees and to make sure they know *how* to prepare one by telling them:

1. It is an overall study of work assignments.

2. It is *not* in any way part of a speed-up program.

Next, have each employee prepare a Task List for a determined period, such as a day or a week. The PMR or research sponsor employee assigned to assist should then:

1. Enter under *hours* the total time spent on each task as accurately as possible.

2. Enter under *volume* the number of units processed or produced for this period. This should be done when the nature of the task makes this possible.

The Task List that is illustrated is a reproduction of one of six actual Task Lists completed by employees of a small materials service division of an equipment maintenance department.

HOW TASK LISTS ARE USED. If a separate Task List is prepared each day for five or more ordinary days, and this is supplemented with notations on activities that occur occasionally or in regular, but varying volume, the PMR will be able to reach conclusions on factors such as skills employed, duplications of review steps, misplaced assignments of supervisory responsibility, and sometimes misconceptions of authority to make decisions and take actions.

A review of Task Lists by the organization supervisor usually clarifies apparent or actual inconsistencies and allows the PMR to share with the supervisor the opportunity to make initial assessments of organizational and operational adequacy. At the same time, this review helps to prepare the supervisor for making further contributions to the success of the review of operations and to adjust to the climate of change that joint study of the Task Lists almost invariably creates.

In studying the illustrative form, the PMR should assume that it was prepared at his/her request and that now he/she must undertake its analysis. He/she should ask himself the following questions, which in actuality should be based on the Task Lists and his own observations of work in progress:

1. Which process takes the most time?
2. Is there any misdirected effort?
3. Are the employees performing too many unrelated tasks?
4. Are tasks spread too thinly?
5. Is there too much specialization or too much generalization?
6. Is the work distributed evenly?
7. Is there a significant volume of peak and valley work?
8. Is there an apparent indication of particularly important skills being at least two deep so that work will continue at a reasonably normal pace during absences?
9. Are there any obvious places where mechanization will pay off in manpower savings or increased promptness in output?
10. Does unaccounted for time exceed six hours per week, exclusive of authorized breaks? If so, why?

Work Distribution Chart

The *Work Distribution Chart* is completed through the use of the Task Lists described under the preceding subtopic heading, and an *Activity List* (not illustrated), which is prepared in collaboration with the organization unit supervisor. The Activity List is merely a summary of all identifiable activities that call for the performance of a number of related tasks. For example, it might be found that almost all employees of the organization unit contribute in some way to the issuance of licenses, which is one of the principal

TASK LIST

☒ PRESENT   ☐ PROPOSED

1st of six lists		POSITION NUMBER 302	POSITION TITLE Section Supervisor (Grade 6)		
DEPARTMENT Equipment Maint.		SECTION Materials Services	UNIT Order Processing		PROJECT NO. 62–79

NUMBER		TASKS	TIME PERIOD	TOTAL PER TASK	
ACTIV.	TASK			HOURS	VOLUME
3	1	Review incoming orders and correspondence	(+) w	10	160
5	2	Expedite orders by telephone	w	8	52
4	3	Review inventory and prepare purchase orders	w	7	32
2	4	Conferences and meetings	w	5	6
1	5	Direct supervision and job instruction (new employees)	w	4	1
8	6	Dictation	w	3	16
7	7	Prepare reports	w	1	1
99	8	Unaccounted for time	w	2	
			w		

(+) w = weeklong test period				TOTALS PER WEEK	40	268

DATE PREPARED 7/23/xx	PREPARED BY Robert Roe	Jane V Roberts REVIEWED BY:	SUPERVISOR	SECTION HEAD James E Jones	DEPARTMENT HEAD A V Smith

WORK DISTRIBUTION CHART

☐ PRESENT
☐ PROPOSED

UNIT CHARTED

NO.	ACTIVITY	HOURS PER WEEK	NAME	Position No	POSITION TITLE	TASKS	HRS PER WEEK	NAME	Position No.	POSITION TITLE	TASKS	HRS. PER WEEK

▲ Left half of form

Right half of form ▼

IF ADDITIONAL COLUMNS ARE REQUIRED, CUT OFF REQUIRED NO. FROM ANOTHER
BLANK FORM AND ATTACH BY PASTING ON TO THE RIGHT EDGE.

| CHARTED BY | DATE | APPROVED BY | | PAGE | OF | PAGES |

NAME	Position No.	POSITION TITLE	TASKS	HRS. PER WEEK	NAME	Position No.	POSITION TITLE	TASKS	HRS. PER WEEK	NAME	Position No.	POSITION TITLE	TASKS	HRS. PER WEEK	TASK HRS. PER WEEK

activities of the unit. Having these facts, the PMR is now ready to place that information on the Work Distribution Chart. If he/she systematically and accurately arranges the information on the chart, he/she will have produced a clear picture of the way the work of the unit is done, and how it is distributed. It will thus be easier to visualize where improvements can be made.

GUIDE TO WORK DISTRIBUTION CHART PREPARATION. To prepare a Work Distribution Chart, use either a specially printed form or a blank sheet of paper on which columns and heading spaces have been ruled in accordance with the example and then—

1. Fill in the top line with as much information as is then available, and leave the remaining space for later completion.
2. Use the first two columns to number and list all the activities, in order of their importance to the fulfillment of the organization's basic mission. In some activities, there may be very little difference between the names assigned. These may be consolidated later if the differences are found to be unimportant, from the work assignment or skill requirements standpoints.
3. Across the top of the chart, enter the names, position titles, and position numbers of the employees involved in carrying out tasks relating to the activities entered in the second column. This should be done by entering the name of the highest grade employee to the left and listing the others toward the right in descending order of position grades or rates of pay.
4. Review each Task List, and identify each task with one of the activities listed in the second column of the chart.
5. Post in the employee's column each of the tasks identified with *activity number one*. For example, assume that the first activity listed in the left-hand column of the Work Distribution Chart is taking inventory. Since this entry was the first one, it should be designated as *No. 1*. All tasks on the individual Task Lists that have to do with taking inventory should have *No. 1* posted adjacent to them. This is done to cross-reference tasks to activity participation by all employees involved.
6. Copy each of the task entries on the Task List onto the Work Distribution Chart opposite the activity, and in the respective columns of the employees who perform the tasks.
7. Record the number of hours and the work count, if available, for each task on the chart.
8. Add the total number of hours spent by all employees for the listed activities across the chart, and enter the total to the right of the name of the activity. Continue this procedure until the chart has been completed.
9. Add the task time entries for each employee and for each activity. The total time for all tasks (added across) should equal the total time worked for all employees (added downward).

HOW WORK DISTRIBUTION CHARTS ARE USED. By following the above steps, the PMR should have a complete and understandable picture of the distribution of work by activities and tasks, currently being performed in the organization. Once the relevant information about the organization is recorded, it is then necessary to analyze the present work distribution and make improvements.

The following questions constitute a guide in analyzing a Work Distribution Chart.

WHAT TASKS TAKE THE MOST TIME?

1. Are all the activities essential to the fulfillment of the unit's mission, or have some been assumed that are unnecessary or done elsewhere?
2. Is the most time devoted to high priority work?
3. Are all necessary operations and tasks included, and is the time spent on each one appropriate?
4. Are activities with component tasks essential to the organization's mission being accomplished?
5. Can work that duplicates work done elsewhere be characterized as misdirected effort?
6. Does study of the administrative and miscellaneous operations disclose any significant amount of misdirected effort?

ARE SKILLS USED PROPERLY?

1. Are skilled employees doing considerable routine work or other tasks that do not use their capabilities sufficiently?

ANALYSIS HINTS RELATED TO THE USE OF EMPLOYEE TIME AND SKILLS.

1. Overloading or underloading employees will result in poor results and lower morale.
2. Aim for a balanced workload among employees.
3. Supervisors and skilled employees should do a minimum amount of routine or other unskilled work.
4. Willing employees may take on work below their skill level.
5. Employees doing work far above their skills usually will do less work of poorer quality and with more accidents, than employees with proper skills.
6. Skilled work should be concentrated in some

positions, and unskilled work in others wherever possible.

ARE EMPLOYEES DOING TOO MANY UNRELATED TASKS?

1. Are some employees performing tasks in every operation?
2. Are willing employees assigned tasks that are unrelated to their normal work?

ANALYSIS HINTS RELATED TO EMPLOYEES USED INDISCRIMINATELY

1. Few people can do all types of work equally well.
2. The assignment of unrelated tasks to employees can result in poorer work, less enthusiasm, and more fatigue.
3. The assignment of related tasks to an employee makes training done to increase skills a lot easier.
4. The willing employee should not be assigned or allowed to assume too many tasks just because of his/her willingness.
5. Tasks may be organized in related groups by types, such as assembling, inspecting, and collecting, and then assigned to appropriate employees.

ARE TASKS SPREAD TOO THIN?

1. Are two or more employees doing small or unimportant tasks one person could do more efficiently?
2. Are some tasks given to so many individuals that no one person is responsible for them?

ANALYSIS HINTS RELATED TO TASK SPREADING

1. If every employee is filing, answering the phone, cleaning the office, or doing similar work, these tasks may be badly performed, and skills may be wasted.
2. One person working steadily usually can accomplish a task more effectively, than many people doing a small part of the same task.

IS WORK DISTRIBUTED EQUITABLY?

1. Are some employees overloaded and others underloaded, or does everyone carry a fair share of the work?
2. Do the tasks of any employee look thin when compared with others?
3. Does the work count information indicate an uneven distribution of work?

ANALYSIS HINTS RELATED TO EQUITABLE WORK DISTRIBUTION.

1. Over a period of a few hours, there are some-times noticeable peaks and valleys in the workers' busyness, which suggests an inequitable distribution of work.
2. Is there a tendency for supervisors to assign the most difficult work to one or two better qualified employees with the result that they are often without sufficient work to keep them busy and are thereby underemployed?

It should be apparent that compiling a Work Distribution Chart such as the one described in this subtopic provides the PMR with a comprehensive, but not necessarily complete, basis for appraising the capability of the organization to accomplish its mission. But the important disclosures are the following:

1. Which activities take the most time
2. Any unessential duplications of supervisory responsibility
3. Any duplications of checking operations
4. Too many levels of supervision
5. Tasks spread too thinly
6. Lack of training for decision making, as reflected in the frequency and time devoted to consulting with superiors on routine tasks or on cases that may have been important in the past but are now obsolete

To summarize, a Work Distribution Chart provides at one time an overall view of the operations performed by the organization unit and exactly who is presently engaged in each type of activity and in what way. It forms the basis, through interviews, study of documents, and comparison of work records, for the PMR to produce a substantial array of relevant assessment comments. For example, if so requested, he/she might propose the following:

1. A training program to raise the level of the routine employees
2. Procedure manuals for the indoctrination of new employees, and as a generally available reference tool for handling unusual situations
3. Rotation of assignments, to ensure two or three days of emergency capability in tasks or positions essential to day-to-day operations
4. Broadening the responsibilities of positions that appear to be overspecialized or spread too thinly over many unrelated tasks
5. Abandonment of functions that this study has disclosed make no contribution, or too little contribution, to achieving the organization's mission

DOCUMENTING ORGANIZATION PLANS

As part of his/her research, the PMR may be called upon to develop a series of specific recommendations and suggestions on how they may be implemented, with or without the research center's assistance. If the T/R that establishes the scope of the research effort provides for this, one of the first obligations of the PMR is to try to reach at least verbal agreement with the research sponsor. To assist him/her with this, he/she may avail himself of various illustrative devices, of which the following will be found to be the most useful.

Organization Charts

An *organization chart* is a graphic means of showing the formal structure of relationships, responsibilities, and authorities through which an organization aims to achieve its objectives. As organizations are constantly changing, there is bound to be a delay between a reorganization that is taking place and its recording on a chart. Therefore, any chart will show the organization only at a given time.

Of all the charts used in management research work, the organization chart is the simplest and most commonly used for describing an organization. It is also the most misunderstood. The frequency with which an organization chart is misunderstood, however, does not destroy its usefulness; it merely indicates the need for explanations and ground rules to govern its use. For example, it is manifestly impossible to illustrate all the relationships existing within and between organizational structures. It is desirable, therefore, to designate exactly what organizational relationships are being illustrated.

While organization charts are easy to read, contain a great deal of information, and are simple to alter as changes become necessary, they have certain disadvantages. They are not very useful for showing duties and responsibilities, except in a general way, such as noting job titles.

Organization charts should be drawn in a simple and consistent manner. While there are many variations, the simplest design is a series of boxes connected by solid lines to indicate chain-of-command relationships between the positions or groups of positions. Any other types of relationships, such as *advisory* relationships characterized by staff officials who provide highly specialized or technical guidance, are best indicated by broken or dotted lines.

There are two commonly used methods of drawing organization charts. The first of these is to use *closed boxes* of various sizes in which are typed position titles, names of persons, or names of organization subunits. The second is to use a typewriter to place lines above and below the titles of positions, the names of persons, or organization subunits and to connect them with vertical and horizontal rows of dots or broken lines. The Conceptual Organization Chart— PMRC in chapter 1 illustrates the most commonly used method of illustrating an organization structure.

Uses of Organization Charts

There are several ways in which organization charts may be used in management studies as follows:

1. As a summary chart of key positions as used in organization guides
2. As a manning table
3. As a detailed working document for showing the names of incumbents of positions
4. As a graphic representation of *functional* relationships
5. As an illustration of the existing organization
6. As a way of communicating to personnel the organization structure and where they fit in it
7. As a help in determining management (supervisory) requirements
8. As an indication of formal lines of communication
9. As an indication of *working* relationships
10. As an indication of formal lines of authority
11. As one of a series of subcharts that provides supporting details relating to a master chart

The first three purposes of organization charts may be their use for showing the names of the incumbents of each position. For salaried positions, there should be a space for the position title, a space for the position number, and a space for the name of the incumbent. When there is more than one identical position reporting to a single higher position, only one space is allowed for the position title, but sufficient space should be provided for however many persons are to be named. Daily rated or labor positions are also shown in summary form, by assigning a box for each group of employees reporting to a single supervisory position. The *number* of daily rated employees in each group is shown as a total in each box, along with their common title.

The other uses of organization charts do not lend themselves to recording names, but are admirably suited to showing *functions* and *activities*.

Advantages and Disadvantages of Organization Charts

The advantages of organization charts in organization analysis and design are that they help to:

1. Identify overlapping functions, jobs, or activities
2. Identify omitted or duplicated functions, jobs, or activities
3. Indicate too many levels of management
4. Indicate spans of control that are too narrow or too wide
5. Indicate lack of unity of command
6. Provide a historical record of changes in the organization
7. Provide induction material for training and a personnel training tool
8. Supply a basis for planning expansion
9. Focus attention on organization weaknesses

The disadvantages of organization charts are the following:

1. They are soon outdated.
2. The cost of preparation and maintenance in an updated condition can be high.
3. They cannot show informal relationships.
4. The relationships shown may not necessarily be those actually in existence.
5. A rigid acceptance of depicted relationships may cause inflexibility, which can impair operating relations.
6. Although published charts should not generally show status, the positions of individuals as depicted may be construed in this manner, leading to status problems.

Charting Prerequisites

When a research project involves consideration of organization structures, the PMR must do the following:

1. Find out if an organization chart or charts already exist.
2. If they exist, determine whether they are up-to-date.
3. If one or more do not exist, construct those required before modifications can be considered.
4. If a chart exists, critically analyze it to determine
   (a) The points noted previously under advantages.
   (b) Whether the structure is as it is required to be, or whether it has been modified to suit the characteristics of personnel available or obtainable.

Types of Organization Charts in Common Use

All types of organization charts have essentially the same advantages and disadvantages, but some of them are clumsier to prepare, and some are more difficult to use in trying to communicate an understanding of organizational relationships and to identify the activities in which the organization is engaged. The following comments will help in reaching a decision on which design is most appropriate.

VERTICAL ORGANIZATION CHART. This is generally recognized as the conventional method of charting both large and small organizations. It typically consists of two or more *layers* of top level executives and/or a board with its subordinate chief executive official. Below that are the operating and staff organizational elements of the agency, each illustrated as a box, or series of boxes, appearing much like an inverted pyramid. Variations in the size of the boxes usually reflect the importance of the position or organization unit. This design is especially suitable when there is to be one *master* chart, supported by a series of more detailed section or unit charts.

VERTICAL ORGANIZATION CHART SHOWING POSITION GRADES. This type of organization chart is essentially the same as the vertical type with the exception that it covers *personnel assignments* rather than organizational elements. Each like position or group of like positions within an organizational element (unit) is placed on the same horizontal level as all other positions of the same grade or salary range. While this presents a somewhat unattractive chart graphically, it is especially useful in manpower studies for showing comparative grades. In this type of chart, the *number* of like positions in each box is usually shown whenever the number exceeds a single position.

HORIZONTAL ORGANIZATION CHART. This type of chart (*see* the Conceptual Organization Chart—PMRC in chapter 1) usually takes up less space than the vertical chart and is useful as an exhibit in a report for that reason. It does not emphasize *status* and is therefore suitable for general circulation.

CONCENTRIC ORGANIZATION CHART. The concentric chart positions the head of the organization in the center, with circles representing levels of authority and sometimes staff relationships. There is no entirely satisfactory way to chart staff relationships, however, other than that that exists between the lower *operating* levels and the higher *direction* level in this type of illustration.

RADIAL ORGANIZATION CHART. This type of chart has very limited use, and can only show the *structural* relationships of the organizational elements. That is, the head of the organization occupies the hub position with all the elements he/she supervises radiating from this central position.

Charting Conventions

All organization charts should be marked with the date of approval, a *title* that states its purpose, and an *exhibit number* if it is to be used as an illustration in a research report. The *name* of the organization charted should also be prominently displayed.

If the PMR's report will be strengthened or better illustrated by a *present* and *proposed* organizational structure, then the style of charts should be the same. For example, for most organization study purposes, a chart showing only the main lines of communication are about all the PMR should attempt to illustrate on one chart.

Such charts in a research report serve the twofold purpose of:

1. Illustrating the present and proposed organization of an agency
2. Acting as a point of additional reference in connection with the arrangement of the report or any organizational deficiencies

It will therefore contribute to the understanding of the narrative that explains the chart if reference is made to that additional coverage in the title of the chart.

In the interest of reducing the amount of manual work in preparing duplication stencils, organization charts can be just as useful and a lot easier to prepare if done on a typewriter, using horizontal lines above and below the names of organization unit, instead of completely surrounding them with a continuous line to make a box. Lines of authority or delegated responsibility should be represented by uninterrupted lines, while lines of consultative communication are drawn with dotted or otherwise broken lines, always explaining the purpose of each in a legend at the bottom of the page.

With practice, charts become easier to draw. Their usefulness is enhanced if they are placed vertically on a single sheet of report paper, rather than horizontally on a gatefold page. If it is necessary to provide more organizational detail than will fit on a single page of report paper, it is best to draw a summary chart that makes reference to an accompanying series of more detailed charts. In all cases, the chart is intended only as a *supplementary aid* to understanding the narrative description of the organization and should never be allowed to take the place of the narrative explanation.

Another aid to understanding an organizational situation is the use of *symbols* to signal changes, such as new positions proposed, new activities, and lines of communication that have been added or deleted. An asterisk or a plus is useful for this purpose.

Organization Manuals

An *organization manual* is the second of the two most frequently used devices for communicating *existing* organizational arrangements, because, unlike organization charts, a manual provides detailed descriptions of key positions, functions, and relationships. It should be noted, however, that organization research projects are more often concerned with existing organizational arrangements than with ways to improve them.

Assuming that the T/R incorporates a provision that the PMRs will offer conclusions about the present organization, and suggestions on appropriate organizational adjustments, the following paragraphs will assist in carrying out such studies. It is also assumed that the T/R calls for a proposed *organization manual* as an end product.

Such a manual should contain detailed position guides for key positions in the organization, and accompanying organization charts. They are usually developed by the PMR in the course of the study, reviewed with the incumbents of the positions, and approved up through the line organization until the senior authority is reached, usually the department head who has the appropriate delegation of authority to issue the manual. Organization manuals are usually issued to a relatively small number of key people, for their use within their organizational units. They are kept up-to-date by revisions sent out as required by the organizational element to which this responsibility has been assigned.

The organization manual is often the most important official document in the agency, since all lower level positions stem from, or derive their authority from, the statements of authority and responsibility it contains. The organization manual, therefore, becomes a most important *authority* control on the organization structure.

Interview Technique in Organization Manual Data Gathering

The interview is the PMR's most important device for gathering information. The PMR's skill, or lack of skill, can often determine the success or failure of an otherwise well-conceived manual development project. Interviewing by the PMR can serve several purposes that will be discussed in the following subtopics.

FACT FINDING. While the interview can be used to gather statistical data, it is equally useful in assessing opinions, morale, attitudes, or thought trends that can be highly significant in formulating conclusions and suggestions.

INFORMING AND MOTIVATING. The interview can be used to acquaint the person being interviewed with new ideas or concepts, or to presell suggestions for better work methods and relationships. A series of well-planned interviews can have extremely useful results in gaining acceptance for change.

APPRAISING. The PMR must continually assess the capabilities of the personnel in the organizational units he/she is studying. Their technical qualifications, intelligence, experience, education, morale, attitudes, proficiency, and achievements will, to a great extent, influence his/her conclusions and suggestions, since a low level of ability and performance may prevent successful installation of new methods, while a high level of ability, achievement, and morale may permit prompt acceptance and speedy implementation of significant changes in an organization.

In spite of what has been said, however, interview may not *always* be the best approach, since interviewing is time-consuming and, unless carefully planned, can be repetitious in terms of information obtained.

Guidelines on When to Use the Interview Technique

1. Use interviews discriminatingly.
2. Make sure the problem to be discussed is significant.
3. Use interviews not only for getting information, but also for gaining the opportunity to observe work areas; appraise personnel; and determine opinions, attitudes, and trends in beliefs.
4. Avoid interviewing for compilation of data of uncertain value or getting general information or commonly known facts.

Preparation for Interviews

Many interviews are not productive because they are not adequately planned. The PMR should consider the following suggestions to ensure better interview results:

1. Decide exactly what the interview is to accomplish. Define the objectives of the interview in advance.
2. Prepare an interview outline in detail with numbered topics. Interview notes can then be readily tied numerically to the corresponding topics in the outline.
3. Know something in advance about the person to be interviewed. If possible, learn about his/her major duties, personality, strengths, and weaknesses.
4. Make appointments. Try to schedule interviews several days, or at least several hours ahead, both as a courtesy and for profitable use of time.
5. Provide for privacy. Consider using a private office where neither party will be interrupted.
6. Consider the interviewee's possible points of view; then examine and discount (without discussing them) your own prejudices.

Observation of the Courtesies and Mechanics of Successful Interviewing

The PMR should observe the following courtesies in conducting his/her interviewing:

1. Be prompt in keeping appointments. If it becomes necessary to make a change, give the interviewee sufficient notice.
2. Respect the property within the office where the interview is to be conducted.
3. Relax, but do not sacrifice good business poise and dignity.
4. Reschedule the interview if unfavorable conditions exist.
5. If the interviewee appears to be under extreme pressure or if he/she is irritable or upset, it is usually better to arrange a later visit.
6. Refrain from smoking if you observe that the interviewee does not smoke; otherwise, ask his/her permission.

The Necessity of Appropriate Introductions

It is essential, particularly at higher levels in the organization, for the PMR to obtain formal introductions. Once introduced to the senior executive in the organization, the PMR should obtain further introductions from this initial contact.

Job Descriptions of Key Officials

When job descriptions are used in organization manuals or otherwise, they are usually limited to only those key positions which will help the user to obtain a clear indication of the division of organizational authority and to point up the levels of that authority in the management of the organization. They, therefore, usually contain a statement of duties and responsibilities and a summary of the qualifications a person filling each key position must have to carry out those duties and responsibilities.

Job descriptions are primarily reference tools and, if not incorporated in a limited circulation operations manual, are often treated as confidential and made available only to those authorized to use them by a top management official.

The principal pitfall in relying on job descriptions for organization analysis and design purposes is the frequency with which they become obsolete. It is important, therefore, for the PMR who uses them as research resources to determine whether they are presently accurate and in force. Otherwise, a considerable amount of time can be wasted in designing an organization structure around what is believed to be accurate information on key job content, lines of communication, etc., when the information is no longer valid.

The drafting of job descriptions, in their final and official form, is usually a *personnel management activity*. For that reason, the drafting of job descriptions by PMRs should not be undertaken, except in unusual circumstances and then, preferably, with the assistance of a skilled personnel analyst.

Standard Procedure Instructions Manuals

A *Standard Procedure Instruction* (SPI) is defined as a written instruction outlining a predetermined course of action. SPIs are intended as guides for people to follow in carrying out repetitive tasks in a systematic, uniform, preplanned way. They are essentially translations of general plans and policies into standard patterns of decision and action. They establish who shall do what, when, and in what sequence.

In some organizations, SPIs are issued individually as need for them emerges. They are then filed either in binders for convenient access or in file folders. Usually, an arrangement system according to related subjects is adopted and, depending on the amount of wear and tear, they are reissued periodically. When this practice is followed, they are reviewed by supervisors and updated to accommodate any procedural changes made since the last update or interim adjustment/addition.

As with the use of job descriptions, obsolescence is a pitfall PMRs must take into account in their use of SPIs. A predetermination should be made of their accuracy and currency, and PMRs should call upon supervisors responsible for updating existing SPIs for assistance here as well. If no SPI manual exists, this subject should be covered by an appropriate suggestion.

EVALUATION OF ORGANIZATIONAL ARRANGEMENTS

The *Organization Arrangements Checklist* incorporates the most essential of the research elements discussed in this chapter. The arrangement of the items listed may be altered and/or modified to fit the peculiarities of the organization under study. In general, however, the PMR will find that if complete information is collected on the items mentioned in this checklist, he/she will have sufficient information to support conclusions and improvement suggestions, with respect to major organizational deficiencies such as inadequate delegations of authority, the grouping of related programs under one leadership, the more complete utilization of available skills, and the more extensive use of employee participation in reaching operating decisions.

ORGANIZATION ARRANGEMENTS CHECKLIST

1. Job descriptions are essential for all personnel except those who share essentially the same duties. These may be prepared for groups as a whole.
2. Base skill assessments on the following:
   a. Qualifications
   b. Tenure in present job
   c. Performance evaluation
   d. Overall knowledge
3. Evaluate work done by each element of the organization in terms of the following:
   a. The intrinsic importance of the work
   b. The formal and informal relationships within the organization
4. Assess the objectives of the organization and each of its subsidiary elements.
5. Assess organization executives with respect to the following:
   a. Responsibilities
   b. Relationships with superiors
   c. Relationships with those supervised
   d. Names and responsibility of any committees to which the executive belongs
   e. Promotability
6. Assess managerial capability with respect to the following:
   a. Are all functions and responsibilities clearly defined?
   b. Is there an organization chart and supplemental (detailed) supporting organization charts?
7. List the Management Committees which have been established.
   a. Are there too many?
   b. Do they stultify decision making?
   c. Do they function through the use of written agendas?
   d. Are they properly run?
   e. Do personal animosities intrude?
   f. What important executive decisions have emanated from them?
   g. What advice or guidance has been passed along by the committees?
8. Observe the strategies and tactics employed to achieve organizational objectives.
9. In the light of the foregoing, highlight any apparent weaknesses in the following areas:
   a. Job responsibility, list any objectives and constraints inherent in each job and indicate where any ambiguities exist.
   b. Are communications poor, adequate, or good?
   c. What working groups exist? Are they productive?
   d. Is the span of control generally delegated to supervisors adequate? Is it too small, adequate, or too great? What factors determine the scope of delegated span of control?
   e. Is there overlapping of suborganizational assignment of functional responsibility? Are consolidations possible?
   f. Line and staff relationships.
   g. Centralization versus decentralization.
   h. Decision making.
   i. Use of committees to study intraorganization and interorganization operating problems.
   j. Function, service, etc., groupings and geographical problems.
   k. Revision need with respect to grades and employee status.
   l. Dissimilar objectives for similar groups of personnel.
   m. Training programs and needs.
   n. Adequacy of controls concerning the following:
      - Expenditures, including capital expenditures.
      - Hiring and firing.
      - Policy decisions.
      - Methods and procedure changes.
   o. Employee morale.
   p. Communications vertically and horizontally.
   q. Standardization (equipment, hours of work, etc.)
   r. Adherence to organization policies.
   s. Flexibility.
   t. Staff utilization of abilities at all levels.
   u. Sufficiency of specialists and specialized assistance.
   v. Frequency and extent of delays.

Chapter 6

THE DATA-GATHERING PROCESS— METHODS AND PROCEDURES STUDIES

THIS CHAPTER IS devoted to discussion and illustration of techniques for improving public management through methods and procedures studies (M&P) and how to apply them.

DEFINITION AND SCOPE OF METHODS AND PROCEDURES STUDIES

The distinctive feature of M&P is their concern with the evaluation of operational standards, procedures, methods, and conventions in the light of the entire public management process. In whatever area this type of research is performed, whether it covers the whole organization or only a part, it should start with a close examination of the objectives of the organization itself. These must be defined with clarity and precision. The research should be concerned with all the processes by which these objectives are achieved, especially the efforts devoted to planning, organization, control, motivation, decision making, and communication. It should also be concerned with the application of techniques by which these processes can be carried out effectively and economically. For these reasons, it is appropriate to introduce M&P research by a working definition, a summary of its scope, and a brief introduction to how M&P are conducted.

Definition

M&P research is a specialized activity that undertakes to improve the efficiency and effectiveness of government through studies of the way operations are conducted. The M&P research function does not have saleable products with which to contend, but rather has products of a different form, its reports, that provide public managers and administrators with the information needed to design and implement improvements. It is not the function of PMRs themselves to undertake the design of improvements unless specifically requested to do so in the T/R that serves as the researcher's charter.

Scope

The scope of M&P research can best be summarized by listing its goals as follow:

1. Simplifying the work and motion patterns on individual jobs
2. Minimizing idle and nonproductive time
3. Balancing line or group operations to obtain maximum utilization of manpower
4. Securing adequate tools and facilities for superior performance of operations
5. Laying out operations and storage facilities for optimum process flow and floor space utilization
6. Developing maximum procedural coordination between related operations and services
7. Introducing mechanization and specialization where economically justified
8. Improving paper work flow procedures
9. Establishing and maintaining standard operation and procedure specifications
10. Minimizing scrap, spoilage and process waste
11. Indoctrinating operating supervisors in the practical application of M&P improvement techniques, such as work simplification
12. Designing new facilities and physical arrangements
13. Locating the causes of excessive operating costs

How Methods and Procedures Studies are Conducted—The Research Project Concept

M&P accomplish most when they begin with a systematic and detailed investigation and analysis process upon which a *findings summary* can be based and its conclusions conveyed to the research sponsor (RS). The principal phases of a M&P research project are discussed next.

Project Planning

Project planning consists mainly of reaching agreement with the RS on what areas are to have particular attention and on which, if any, operational areas are to be given less detailed study because of contemplated program change or any other reason. When the T/R is fully understood by all concerned, assigning research staff, appointing a liaison officer from the RS staff, and timing contemplated research project phases can be reduced to written statements and/or staff assignment charts. This process usually consists of fact finding and recording.

FACT FINDING. The first step is to ascertain the facts, with the objective of determining all available methods and procedural facts relating to the operations under study. To obtain facts, the cooperation of all concerned must be secured.

RECORDING THE FACTS. The facts must then be recorded in an orderly and easily discernible manner. There are several ways of doing this. For example, charting techniques, modeling, and photography are especially useful. The choice of technique depends on the type of material. The objective is always to present the findings in an easily understandable manner for purposes of examination.

Critically Analyzing the Facts

Facts should be critically analyzed to arrive at conclusions. There are many techniques that can be used at this stage, ranging from simply analyzing the results of face-to-face interviews, to advanced mathematical modeling.

Reporting the Findings and Conclusions

Findings and conclusions should be reported and, if requested, structural plans or methods and procedures suggestions submitted to the RS.

The foregoing requirements for a successful M&P research project, when considered in their totality, can be characterized as the *PMR Project Concept*.

PLANNING AND SCHEDULING METHODS AND PROCEDURES STUDIES

M&P must be based on a sound plan developed through observations and consultations with the RS operation and staff departments, to determine and agree upon areas that need improvement. The first task is to select problems for study. There may, for example, be bottlenecks, excessive supplies costs, ineffective use of manpower and equipment, poor maintenance, unsafe or difficult working conditions, lack of communication, and many other operational deficiencies.

To make the most effective use of RS personnel and ensure an orderly and systematic approach to the development of M&P improvements, it is wise to plan a continuing schedule of projects well in advance of the actual studies. The planning and preparation of a study schedule should be based on the following:

1. *Consultations* with the RS line supervisors and staffs regarding operating problems that limit output and offer the greatest cost reduction possibilities.
2. *Study of monthly activity reports* and financial statements on productivity and the distribution of costs for each division and/or department. It is sometimes necessary for the PMR to help design such reports and statements.
3. *Discussion of methods with operating personnel* in the various departments in which plans are being made, for example, for the installation of new equipment, changes in design or layout of existing equipment and facilities, the use of available work areas, or the utilization of services provided by others.
4. *Rapport* between the senior PMRC professional staff and the RS line supervisors should be established, since it is the latter who are directly responsible for the overall efficiency of day-to-day operations. Those areas which the line supervisors consider the most critical should receive high priority in the planning of the M&P schedule. The PMRC should perform its functions at those points at which line supervisors feel they can be most effectively utilized; however, the director of the PMRC should also suggest projects for study, based on his/her own observations of the RS operations.

GATHERING AND VERIFYING METHODS AND PROCEDURES DATA

Each M&P usually presents a different problem in the gathering of data.

Background Data

Much of the needed information may already be available in the form of regulations, specifications, standard procedures, organization guides, time studies, and operational reports. Complete information on present M&Ps should be acquired in order to provide a basis of comparison with any proposed methods and procedures changes. Furthermore, as a necessary preliminary step in the M&P, the PMR should check and review any studies made on similar operations in other parts of the organization, including studies by outside agencies.

It is also important for the PMR to review professional journals and technical papers having a bearing on the activity under study. These frequently have valuable technical information pertaining to the M&P.

Observation of Present Methods

The PMR will obtain his/her most useful information through his/her own careful observation and study of present methods and procedures. Pertinent past history, many relevant facts, and some new ideas may be (and usually are) obtained in this way. Information collected about the tasks involved in a procedure may include data such as descriptions of equipment, materials, personnel requirements, operating sequence, and methods. Data relating to productivity, such as past performance, source of materials, and costs, are also important facts about the procedures and methods presently employed. Detailed facts relating to the various steps involved in performing the tasks must be gathered, as well as facts regarding the flow of information and the use of manpower, materials, facilities, and equipment. Finally, if an activity involves several employees working on different phases of any operation, it may be necessary to collect facts about them as a whole, as well as individually and in relation to one another.

Verification of Facts

The information obtained should be verified as to its accuracy, completeness, timeliness, and adequacy. Information obtained through *conversations* with individuals should also be checked through two or more sources for accuracy and completeness. Any inconsistencies should be noted and reconciled. The source and date should be noted, and all data recorded in an orderly manner and filed for easy reference.

RECORDING METHODS AND PROCEDURES INFORMATION

Of the several methods used for recording M&P data, the most common are as follow:

1. Procedure analysis charts
2. Document route charts
3. Procedure diagrams
4. Multiple-activity charts

Each of these is discussed later in this chapter. They may all be used to follow material, people, or records as they move within a work process. Often it is desirable to supplement the information on charts with scale models of machines and equipment or by the use of still or motion photography.

A study of such charts should suggest possibilities for the elimination of inefficiencies. Information, such as distance that documents or materials travel and the time for completing operations, may be included to permit a comprehensive and detailed analysis of all work processes. The actual observation required to gather the data for such graphics usually discloses opportunities for improvement.

The only tools needed by the PMR to make adequate graphic illustrations to support M&P reporting are a pencil; a ball-point pen; a ruler; a 25 meter (or equivalent) tape measure; a good quality eraser; a 35 mm camera with medium speed black and white film; a template for drawing symbols on charts, such as those described next; a notebook; and a supply of paper for drafting and illustrating reports on M&P improvement findings.

The charts and forms described or illustrated in the following pages may be printed, if there is a sufficient volume of work to justify this expense. Because charts tend to become cluttered through the constant need to revise the data on them, the use of hand-ruled and typewritten forms, rather than printed forms, is generally satisfactory.

Extensive use of many different designs has proved it is desirable for the PMR to be conversant with at least the following types of charts and able to modify them as freely as necessary to meet individual preferences and needs. The important thing is not to *force* too much information on one chart.

It will be observed that in some respects, the four forms discussed in the following pages, as well as the Task List and the Work Distribution Chart that were discussed in the preceding chapter, serve some of the same purposes. This is because each may serve one or more uses, but not always as readily or as completely, as the others.

Procedure Analysis Chart

There is a class of operational problems that results from the flow of a particular *system* through a number of work stations. A M&P is a systematic examination of the whole work flow in a complete system. This type of study ignores those aspects of an organization's activities which do not bear directly on the system being studied. The study may involve several people in a work center, or in several work centers. The focus of a M&P is on the *work steps* involved in a specific operation that may require the efforts of several persons or groups to complete.

Procedure Analysis Charts provide a detailed breakdown in symbolic and summary narrative form of a series of interrelated events. This chart is prepared by recording, in sequence and in detail, all steps under study, using the appropriate chart symbols. Depending on the purpose of the chart, other information such as operations performed, distance moved, transportation, idle time, costs, and other details may be recorded through the use of symbols or in the form of short narrative statements.

Guide to Procedure Analysis Chart Preparation

A series of seven standardized symbols has been developed to assist PMRs in describing work flow. They and their uses are illustrated in Figure 1.

With these symbols in mind, the PMR then

1. Chooses definite points to start and end the cycle of steps to be analyzed. He/she includes only elements that pertain to M&P.
2. While observing actual conditions, he/she describes each step clearly and concisely in brief statements that start with an action verb, such as follow:
   a. Types letter
   b. Walks to duplicator
   c. Checks spelling
   d. Telephones secretary
3. Makes sure no steps are omitted or combined.
4. Shows distance in meters or feet for each transportation step.
5. Opposite each step, shows the number of units of each item handled or personnel involved,

and the time required in minutes.
6. Tentatively indicates for each step, the *possibilities* for improvement, in the left-hand column heading (if this is called for in the T/R).
7. Summarizes the information in the spaces provided in the upper section of the form.

Statements should be short and descriptive so that the PMR can graphically and/or verbally reconstruct the procedure at a later time. It should be detailed enough to diagram the actual operation, using a *Procedure Diagram* that is described and illustrated later in this chapter.

All element descriptions should be checked by observing a second cycle of the actual on-the-spot operation, being sure that all distances are measured, and that the time obtained for the duration of all procedural steps is confirmed. When the foregoing tasks have been completed, the sequence of all the work steps required to complete the total procedure is traced by joining the symbols that represent the seven categories of activity with *solid lines* and *shading* those symbols that are thus joined. The recorded sequence of steps thus portrayed enables visualization of the entire chain of events, the relationships of the various elements to each other, and the steps required to complete the procedure.

How Procedure Charts are Used

A detailed analysis of the chart described above is first made by studying the inputs and outputs of the procedure. This analysis attempts to differentiate between the inputs and outputs required by the nature of the system but does not, at this point, include reaching conclusions concerning steps that are not logically necessary. The initial analysis of inputs and outputs is followed by a determination and evaluation of the work time and volume of output for each step under the *present* system. All steps of the system are then analyzed in depth to locate specific opportunities for improvements. It is at this point in the analysis that the researcher's analytical, creative, and innovative capabilities are put to the test. Tentative ideas concerning improvements will have been

PROCEDURE ANALYSIS CHART SHEET NO.

☒ MAN	☐ MATERIAL	☐ EQUIPMENT	(name of organization)

JOB ☒ PRESENT ☐ PROPOSED
Processing of routine correspondence

Starting when morning mail reaches office

and terminates with last mail pickup.

DEPT./LOCATION
Department of Social Affairs & Labor

CHARTED BY A.R.S. **DATE** 5/12/xx

SUMMARY

METHOD	PRES.	PROPD.	SAVG.
NO. OF OPERATIONS	19		
NO. OF TRANSPORTATIONS	16	64 steps	
NO. OF INSPECTIONS	4		
NO. OF DELAYS	24		
NO. OF SHORTAGES	1		
MINUTES	190		
DISTANCE TRAVELLED	285ft.		

STEPS	WHAT - job, person, operation, material, form? WHERE - done, moved, inspected, delayed, stored? WHEN - day, month, year, deadline, peak load?	OPERATION	TRANSPOR.	INSPECTION	DELAY	STORAGE	FEET	MINUTES	Eliminate Combine Simplify Rearrange
1	Mail arrives at main door of department office						6	2	Rearrange delivery time
2	Mail received by chief mail clerk or deputy							1	Eliminate by use of trapdoor
	awaits arrival of mail clerk							3	
	and sorted by mail clerk								
15	Folder awaits							3	Eliminate step
16	Folder awaits pickup by messenger							3	Rearrange sched.
									◄ BROUGHT FORWARD
	Continued on following page	7	6	0	9	0	88	78	◄ TOTALS

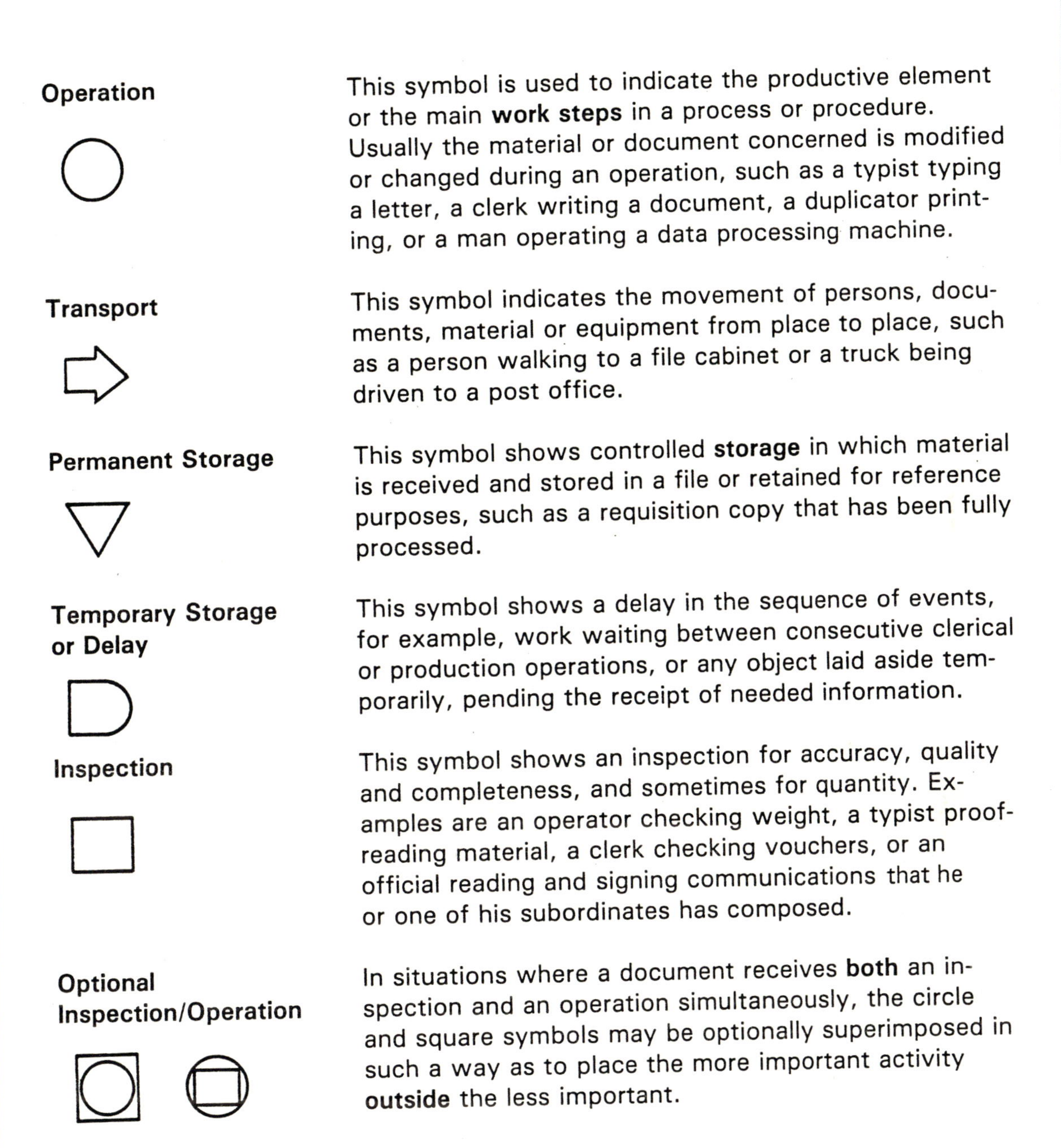

Figure 1. Standardized Symbols used to illustrate procedure flow.

noted in the right-hand column by using any one of the following:

1. Eliminate
2. Combine
3. Simplify
4. Rearrange

If the PMR thinks it will help to develop conclusions or to cite specific improvement suggestions, he/she should use the (chart) line number as a reference and make notes of his/her improvement conclusions and/or suggestions on separate pages.

In making this type of study the PMR should refer to other completed forms that may have relevance, such as follow:

1. *Tasks Lists* (*see* chapt. 5) are useful, for identifying specific tasks and functions directly related to the system under study.
2. *Work measurement records*, time studies, and work sampling summaries, may disclose productivity situations and suggestions made at another time for improvements.

From the foregoing, it should be apparent that the *Procedure Analysis Chart* is actually a breakdown of the elements of each individual task or operation. Its purpose is to gain more intimate knowledge of individual procedural steps as follows:

1. By *recording* the detailed work pattern and movements of a document, the things the employee must know or watch for, the conditions that affect the operation and the time of such movements, the PMR should gain all the information required by an employee to perform his/her job assignment satisfactorily.
2. The *degree of refinement* to be attained in analyzing the work pattern is determined largely by the nature of the operation and the manpower costs involved.
3. When the *pertinent facts* regarding the operation have been gathered and assembled, the next step is to consider every detail. Successful analysis can only be accomplished by thorough questioning. No phase of the existing method or procedure can be taken for granted. There is almost always a better way. Questions must not be asked at random. Systematic questioning is just as important as systematic data gathering by any other means.
4. Every question that can reasonably be asked is raised in a logical fashion in order to query the task as a whole and then each detail of the operation is queried in the following manner:
   a. *What* is done? Why is it necessary? What is its purpose?
   b. *Where* is it done? Why is it done there? Where should it be done?
   c. *When* is it done? Why is it done then? When should it be done?
   d. *Who* does it? Why does that person do it? Who is the best qualified and best positioned person to do it?
   e. *How* is it done? Why is it done this way? Is there a better way of doing it?

To reiterate, the *Procedure Analysis Chart* is used to discover opportunities to

1. Simplify the operation through combining or eliminating inspection steps.
2. Relocate personnel so that those who take successive procedural steps are in close proximity.
3. Introduce new time- and effort-saving methods, such as the use of office machines, combining process steps, introducing one-time writing methods, and using lower grade skills and multipurpose forms. There is literally no end to the number and variety of ways to simplify operational systems.

Having discovered opportunities for systems improvement, any proposed changes, if so required in the T/R, are measured against present operations by turning to the Procedure Analysis Chart in which each step to be revised has been noted in the four right-hand columns. Any steps proposed for complete elimination are also identified. With this information on hand, a *Proposed Procedure Analysis Chart* is prepared. The *present* and *proposed* numbers of each type of step, time lapses, and distances are then entered in the spaces provided for this purpose in the summary box at the top of the first page of the *proposed* chart.

A brief narrative statement (if so required) of the purpose of the revised operating procedure, the benefits that will accrue if it is adopted, and what action must be taken to implement the changes should take the form of either a memorandum to the head of the RS organization or be incorporated in a more formal report.

Present and proposed Procedure Analysis Charts, like those just described, were prepared during a study of the procedure followed by a government agency in replying to routine inquiries directed to its department of social welfare. The study produced the astonishing (to the RS) information that sixty-four steps were involved, requiring an average of 3.6 days (mostly traceable to delays) and over 286 meters of travel within the department's medium-sized office building. A careful analysis of matters such as operating methods, delegations of authority, regulations, and the causes of delay resulted in a revised procedure that reduced the number of steps to thirty, the distances traveled to 136 meters, and the elapsed time to 1.2 days. A new procedure that delegated increased authority to supervisors to take prompt and independent action, and several new *form letters* and *standard paragraphs* were introduced for use in replying to often-received inquiries.

Document Route Chart

A *Document Route Chart* (not illustrated) is simply a series of three- or four-inch columns across a work sheet headed with the names of either individuals, positions, or the names of functional organization units within the activity being studied. The form should be headed to indicate the organization element or elements being studied, the date of the study, a note that it is the *present* procedure that is shown, and who did the charting.

A *Document Route Chart* is especially useful in demonstrating that a large amount of document handling and repetitive writing of information onto a whole series of related forms can be avoided if those forms are designed in order to meet *multiple* needs. A saving of time, effort, and the possibility of error is the usual result. This is especially so in cases in which RS personnel who are engaged in the use of the forms being analyzed are assisting PMRS. It is also useful in connection with procedures that call for the use of several different forms or copies of forms that circulate widely through the organization. Its principal use, therefore, is in connection with winning support for change and in gaining help in deciding what M&P and forms-consolidation changes should occur.

Guide to Document Route Chart Preparation

The Document Route Chart is completed through the use of single forms and all sections of multi-part forms that are completed or utilized in one or more separate, but interdependent, procedures. The emphasis here is on improving the design of forms to eliminate unnecessary writing of the same information, and to reduce the error hazard thus created.

When the PMR intends to incorporate a Document Route Chart in his report, a template may be used to illustrate the original and all copies of the forms employed. Alternatively, conventional symbols, such as those shown on the Procedure Analysis Chart, may be used. Arrows are drawn to indicate the distribution of all copies of each form sent from one person or organizational unit to another. Brief notations are made to indicate the information added, taken from, or checked for accuracy at each point along the flow of documents between units.

How the Document Route Chart is Used

By observing what happens to various copies of the form as the procedure progresses, it is easy for the PMR to detect duplications of information adding, checking effort, unused or poorly arranged information, and other deficiencies. To illustrate, the main use of the Document Route Chart is to demonstrate to users as follows:

1. Whether a need exists to collaborate in the redesign of forms that serve multiple purposes.
2. Where unnecessary information can be omitted.
3. That some present users need not have file copies but can meet all necessary obligations by using a circulating copy of the form.
4. How actual copies of forms can be used as permanent records, rather than copying information into other types of information storage facilities, such as ledgers and registers.

A Document Route Chart was prepared in connection with the acquisition of spare parts for a department of public works fleet of trucks and construction equipment. The result of that particular study was that by designing a multi-copy, snapout form, all needs for information on requisitioning, authority to purchase, ordering, delivery inspection reporting, vouchering for payment of vendor, and payment transmittal purposes could be met through a single writing of the identifying and commodity specification information. This single-writing method accomplished the following:

1. Eliminated six other forms
2. Reduced the paper-processing steps in the procedure by about 48 percent
3. Speeded-up the overall lapse of time between requisitioning and delivery of commodities by approximately 40 percent
4. Served as the basis for introducing changes in purchasing regulations that resulted in significant economies as well as eliminating some suspected opportunities to collaborate in the payment of *kickbacks* by dishonest vendors

Where and How Deficiencies can be Corrected

Forms should be arranged on the Document Route Chart to reflect the paths copies follow in the *present* and *proposed* procedures. It is preferable, however, to support the chart with a narrative that explains where critical savings can be made, where duplication of effort is most serious in terms of error potential and in costs of clerical time, and where copies of forms are wastefully provided.

To summarize, the foregoing discussion of the Document Route Chart completes the series of charts that are, to a greater or lesser degree, prepared through the use of information that came to the PMR through a Task List such as that described and illustrated in chapter 5. To reiterate, the following points are worthy of emphasis:

1. Because Task Lists serve as a key source of information on operating procedures, they should be prepared and subsequently analyzed, summarized, and cross-referenced with great care.
2. The PMR will find, through experience, that

operational deficiencies show up more completely and certainly if the forms involved and the actual tasks performed, or mechanical equipment used, are made visible through some form of chart. This allows quick reference from one operation to the others, and the PMR's discussion is not interrupted by having to locate related documents in order to show in what respects they can be improved.

3. The discovery of operating deficiencies represents only about 20 percent of the PMR's responsibility. The other 80 percent comes in designing improved operations, convincing the RS that estimates of cost and other savings are valid and worth the effort that must be made to effect changes, and in appropriate circumstances, participating in the implementation of M&P improvements.

Procedure Diagram

Procedure Diagrams are sketches of work areas drawn to scale that show where each phase of an operating procedure occurs. The Procedure Diagram is really a worksheet, designed for convenient use by a PMR in noting the measured distances between work places. The form is also suitable for illustrating a final project report that, of necessity, must be in a convenient size and capable of duplication.

If the M&P's T/R calls for conclusions and suggestions on how office or other work center improvements can be made, two charts should be prepared. The first chart should be labeled *present*, and the second should be labeled *proposed* and be accompanied by a narrative that identifies and evaluates the benefits of the new procedure.

Another Procedure Diagram format that is ideally suited for illustrating present and proposed arrangements to members of the RS staff at a conference or in giving instructions to RS personnel generally is the use of a large cork board, a metal panel, or a sheet of some other material onto which can be attached scale drawings or cutouts of desks, cabinets, office machines, etc., with colored string connecting the several steps of the diagrammed procedure. To prevent confusion, occasional arrows should also be used to indicate the direction of procedure (document) movements.

A floor plan of the entire area without any markings may also be used in situations in which it is important to show the movement of people, documents, etc., from one place to another within the

work area under study. Then, by superimposing successive sheets of tracing paper over this floor plan, each separate procedure may be illustrated in different colored lines, with arrows used to indicate the direction of paperwork movement. When the separate procedure diagrams are superimposed on each other and the basic floor plan, the extent of congestion in passageways and the disturbance caused by excessive movement of people will become clear, as will the distances traveled in the course of procedure operations and the remoteness of supervisors, in many cases, from those whom they supervise.

In the event that a procedure diagram covering *two or more* procedures is to be duplicated for a final report and must be presented in black and white, a series of hand-drawn and typewritten lines can be used, such as follow:

```
————————————————————felt tip pen
————————————————————ball-point pen
— — — — — — — — — —ball-point pen
------------------------------------typewriter
- - - - - - - - - - - - - - - - - - -typewriter
- -- -- -- -- -- -- -- -- -- -- --typewriter
.............................typewriter
* * * * * * * * * * * * * * * * * *typewriter
= = = = = = = = = = = = = = = =typewriter
```

If work areas are located on different floors of a building, it may be necessary to prepare two or more Procedure Diagrams, being careful to show all connecting points and directions of movement. An alternative to this is to make a three-dimensional floor

PROCEDURE DIAGRAM
(Before and After Office Layout Study)

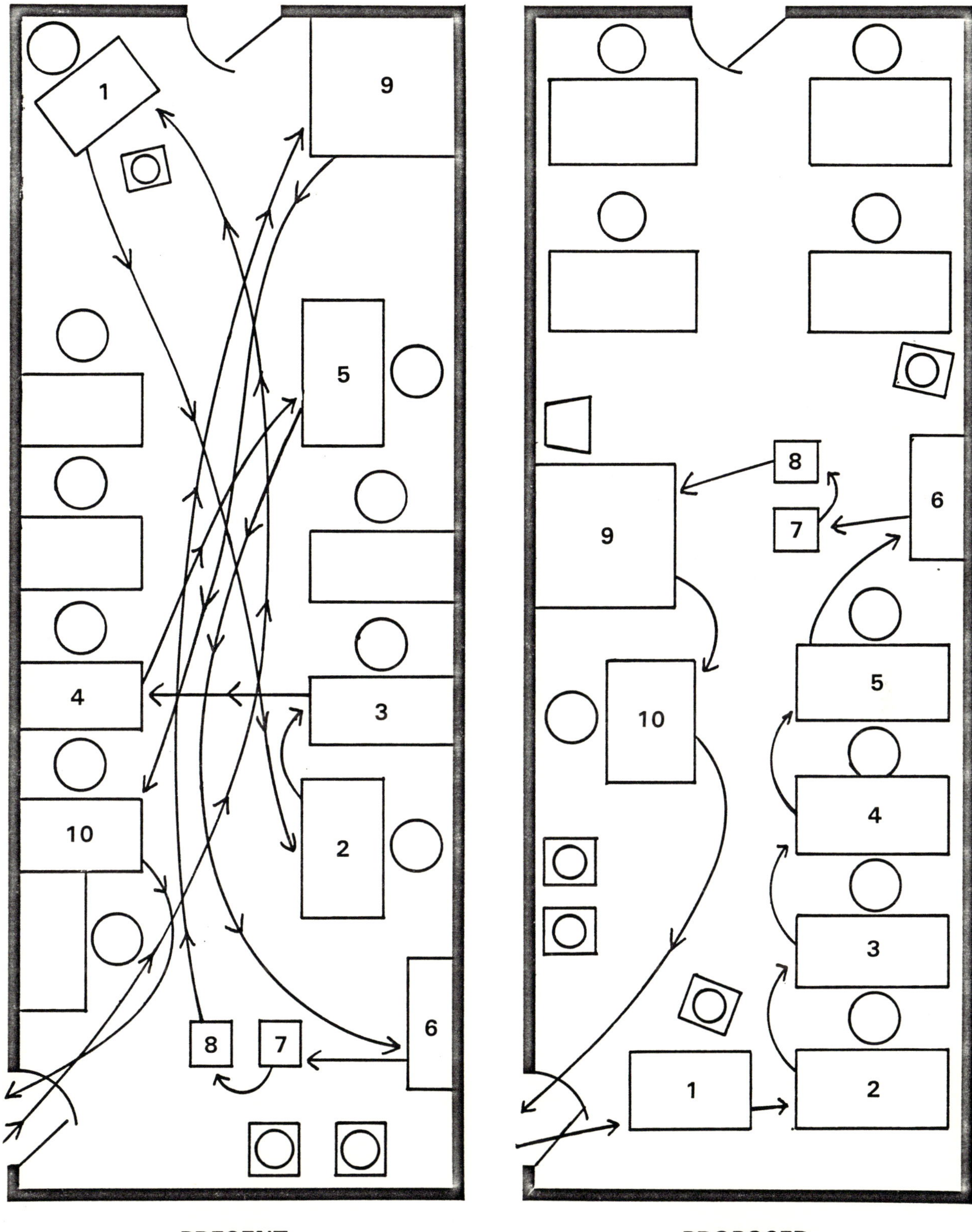

plan of each work area, drawn in perspective and using colored or broken lines to indicate movement routes.

Guide to Procedure Diagram Preparation

The preceding paragraphs are confined to the *purpose* of Procedure Diagrams and a diagram format. The following explains how such diagrams are prepared after the matter of format has been settled.

As it is the purpose of a Procedure Diagram to illustrate the relationship between work places, work centers, and work areas in fulfilling procedural requirements, action symbols, such as those used on the Procedure Analysis Chart described earlier, should be used. A typical *Procedure Diagram* is illustrated. Sometimes the circle, square (or a combination of them), triangle, arrowhead, and *D* are placed at each work place, such as a desk, that is in any way involved in the procedure under analysis. Within each such symbol may be written a number referring to a numbered note or comment on a separate worksheet concerning each procedural activity. When it is more convenient to do so, however, encircled *task* numbers may be used instead of action symbols. The same numbers would normally be used in connection with the procedure notes dealing with any procedural changes, such as the following:

1. The relocation of the unit supervisor from one end of the room to the other
2. The locations of Task 7 and Task 8
3. The moving of the stamping machine (location 6) from one end of the room to the other.

The net effect of this rearrangement of task positions reduced the distance traveled by license applications from 221 feet to 128 feet and provided a better supervisory vantage point. It should be noted also in connection with the Procedure Diagram that no number was assigned to the desks located at the upper end of the room because they were used only occasionally by field inspectors whose duties were not covered by the diagrammed procedure.

If the procedure being diagrammed by the PMR is especially complicated, it is best to use two diagrams or to put the *proposed* procedure (if required by the T/R) on semi-transparent paper and use it as an overlay.

To summarize, the following are the most important considerations in the preparation of Procedure Diagrams, whatever their format:

1. Indicate all the basic events concerned with the procedure under study.
2. Draw the diagram to scale whenever possible.
3. Emphasize the *flow lines* and *basic events*. The outline of buildings and other items should be drawn in lighter lines.
4. When the Procedure Diagram is used in conjunction with a Procedure Analysis Chart, always mark with the appropriate symbol each point on the flow lines where an operation, transportation, inspection, storage, or delay occur.
5. Show the sequence of events by writing the relevant step number inside the symbol.
6. At the bottom of each page, summarize the most important activities, and, if the T/R statement requires, note the differences that might be introduced between the present and the proposed work center arrangements.

How Procedure Diagrams are Used

Scrutiny of the *present* Procedure Diagram represents the most important phase in this type of M&P study. This scrutiny is most easily accomplished if the PMR asks himself, and any RS personnel who might be assisting in the study, four questions about each of the five related aspects of the procedure under analysis;

1. *Purpose*—What is done? Why is it done? What else might be done? What should be done?
2. *Place*—Where is it done? Why is it done there? Where else might it be done? Where should it be done?
3. *Sequence*—When is it done? Why is it done then? When might it be done? When should it be done?
4. *Person*—Who does it? Why does that person do it? Who else might do it? Who should do it?
5. *Means*—How is it done? Why is it done that way? How else might it be done? How should it be done?

With this information in hand, the PMR will be in an excellent position, if the T/R specifies, to select the types of changes that *might* help to do the following:

1. Achieve shorter and less repetitive travel over the same routes (i.e., eliminate backtracking)
2. Find duplicate *checking* steps
3. Combine procedural activities by the same or different personnel
4. Relocate any of the work centers to achieve greater convenience for those concerned, shorter travel distances, and better supervision in the interest of improved productivity
5. Eliminate any procedural steps not essential to the proper working of the system
6. Modify the sequence of procedural steps to

permit taking two or more to the same place without intervening travel or checking/inspection steps.

Having carried out this analysis of *present* operations, the PMR is in a position to start what can best be described as a series of experiments, to see if any or all of the *findings* enumerated above can be merged into a *proposed* procedural routing scheme. If it can, a second copy of the Procedure Diagram should be marked *proposed* and filled out by applying the appropriate symbols, step numbers, task notations, etc., for comparison with the *present* Procedure Diagram.

It should not be assumed that the acknowledgement of work flow deficiencies is a guarantee that any suggestions to overcome them will be promptly and enthusiastically implemented. Reactions are quite the contrary in cases in which, for example, a RS staff member with long tenure is asked to move from his preferred location or in which someone defends his claim to a location because it is close to a piece of office equipment he uses *occasionally*. It is not the function of the PMR to arbitrate disagreements as to where personnel shall be located.

Multiple Activity Chart

In concluding this discussion of M&P charts, it should be emphasized that with the exception of the Task List and the Work Distribution Chart, the charts so far discussed in this chapter deal with *individual* procedures. It is sometimes difficult to draw a readily understandable chart covering two or more procedures that are implemented simultaneously even when the same person or the same kinds of duties are involved. The best method of portraying related or supplementary procedures is to use the same design for all charts intended to disclose related operating situations and to make comparisons between them only when this will serve a purpose, such as pointing out unwarranted duplications of skills being employed separately by different persons in the same or different locations.

Illustrated are two types of *Multiple Activity Charts*. The first (A) illustrates the use of brief *notations* on the tasks performed, while the second (B) uses conventional activity symbols to identify the types of activities performed. If activity symbols are used, it is not essential to supply descriptive words as well.

Usually, the activities are recorded in the form of notations that identify and describe the meaning of vertical bars so that the final record becomes a *Multiple Bar Chart*. The lengths of the vertical bars are subdivided against the time scale in the left margin of the form, according to the duration of the activity they represent. The data for the chart can be gathered from on-the-spot time studies. Movies of clerical and production operations have also been the source of data on multiple activities.

The Multiple Activity Chart is often time-consuming to prepare and use, but it is an excellent tool for spotting ineffective ways of performing work and utilizing time, such as the following:

1. Idle time—person waiting for person
2. Idle time—machine waiting for person

3. Too much manpower—one person waiting for another *to get out of the way*
4. Poor distribution of tasks—one employee overworked, another doing nothing
5. Poor layout—long transport

This particular way of representing a procedure graphically is also useful when parallel charts are exhibited that illustrate present and proposed ways of handling multiple activities.

Guide to Preparing Multiple Activity Charts

Because of the relative infrequency with which Multiple Activity Charts are used in M&P, it is usually preferable to draw them rather than to have them printed. Irrespective of whether the chart is drawn or printed, it is prepared as follows.

PURPOSE AND SCOPE OF CHART. Define the purpose and scope of the activities to be charted, and provide a separate column for each involved person.

POSITION OF ACTIVITIES ON THE CHART. As the purpose of the chart is to analyze the coordination (or lack of coordination) of several activities, the elemental subdivision must be placed in the area opposite the *time scale* (representing the duration of the process) at which that activity falls within the cycle. In this way, a visual record is constructed to show the interrelationship of the activities of the person or persons and machines engaged in the process. An adequate description of the activities represented must be provided to do the following:

1. Show idle time and working time separately.
2. Make sure no short periods of *work* are included in *idle time*, and vice versa.
3. Make clear which method the chart represents—present or proposed.

DURATION OF ACTIVITY. The start and finish of a cycle represented on the chart must be specifically indicated.

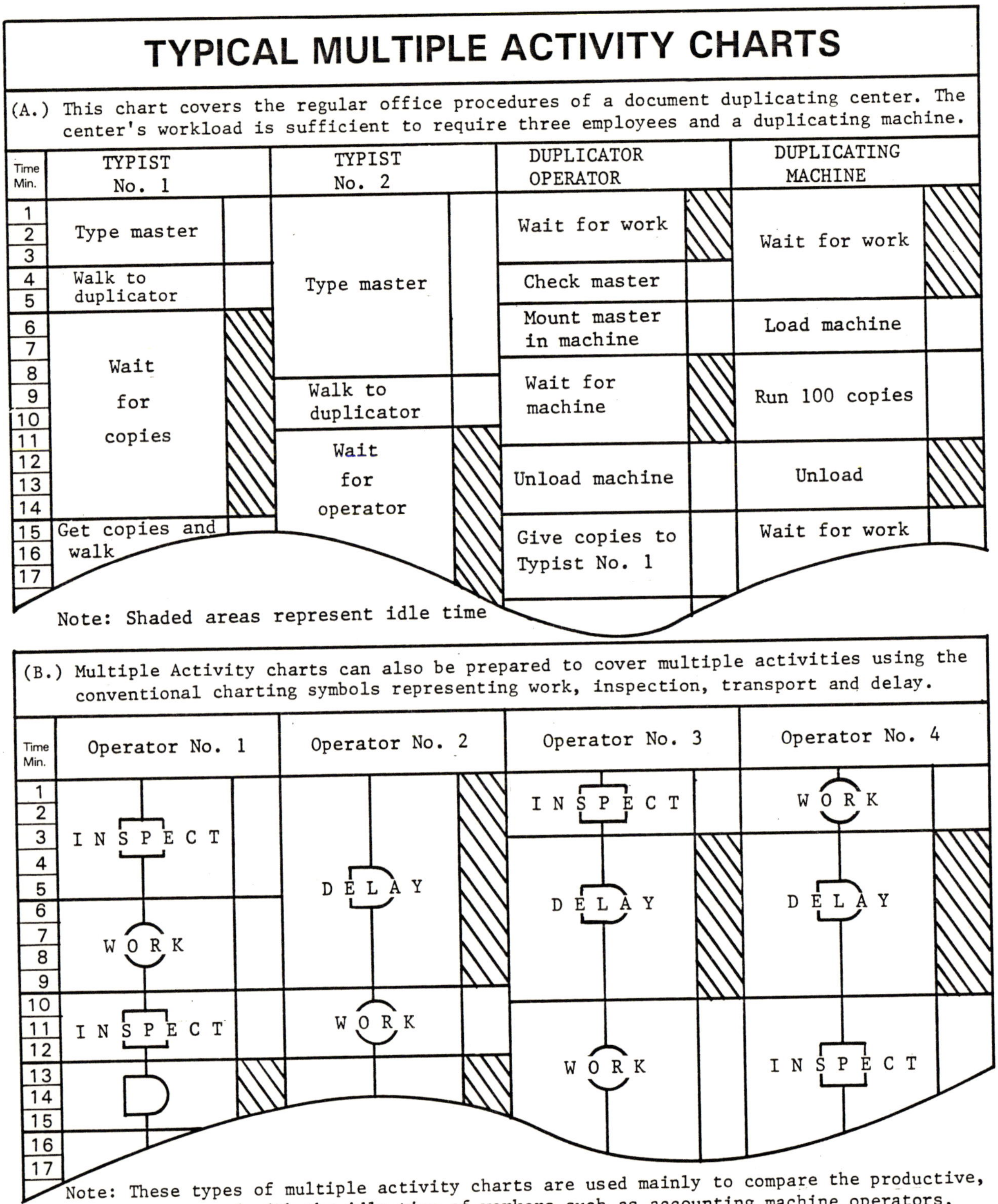

Public Management Research

TYPICAL MULTIPLE ACTIVITY CHARTS

(A.) This chart covers the regular office procedures of a document duplicating center. The center's workload is sufficient to require three employees and a duplicating machine.

Time Min.	TYPIST No. 1	TYPIST No. 2	DUPLICATOR OPERATOR	DUPLICATING MACHINE
1	Type master		Wait for work	Wait for work
2	Type master		Wait for work	Wait for work
3	Type master		Wait for work	Wait for work
4	Walk to duplicator	Type master	Check master	Load machine
5	Walk to duplicator	Type master	Check master	Load machine
6	Wait for copies	Type master	Mount master in machine	Load machine
7	Wait for copies	Type master	Mount master in machine	Load machine
8	Wait for copies	Walk to duplicator	Wait for machine	Run 100 copies
9	Wait for copies	Walk to duplicator	Wait for machine	Run 100 copies
10	Wait for copies	Walk to duplicator	Wait for machine	Run 100 copies
11	Wait for copies	Wait for operator	Unload machine	Unload
12	Wait for copies	Wait for operator	Unload machine	Unload
13	Wait for copies	Wait for operator	Unload machine	Unload
14	Wait for copies	Wait for operator	Unload machine	Unload
15	Get copies and walk	Wait for operator	Give copies to Typist No. 1	Wait for work
16	Get copies and walk		Give copies to Typist No. 1	Wait for work
17				

Note: Shaded areas represent idle time

(B.) Multiple Activity charts can also be prepared to cover multiple activities using the conventional charting symbols representing work, inspection, transport and delay.

Time Min.	Operator No. 1	Operator No. 2	Operator No. 3	Operator No. 4
1	INSPECT	DELAY	INSPECT	WORK
2	INSPECT	DELAY	INSPECT	WORK
3	INSPECT	DELAY	INSPECT	WORK
4	INSPECT	DELAY	DELAY	DELAY
5	INSPECT	DELAY	DELAY	DELAY
6	WORK	DELAY	DELAY	DELAY
7	WORK	DELAY	DELAY	DELAY
8	WORK	DELAY	DELAY	DELAY
9	WORK	DELAY	DELAY	DELAY
10	INSPECT	WORK	WORK	INSPECT
11	INSPECT	WORK	WORK	INSPECT
12	INSPECT	WORK	WORK	INSPECT
13			WORK	INSPECT
14				
15				
16				
17				

Note: These types of multiple activity charts are used mainly to compare the productive, as compared with the idle time of workers such as accounting machine operators, who engage in essentially the same tasks on a highly repetitive basis.

DEFINITION OF TIME SCALE. There are alternatives available to the PMR in establishing the time scale according to which elapsed time can be measured. The first is in minutes, while the second is a metric measurement of six minutes, which represents 10 percent of an hour and is much easier to calculate, but not as easy as minutes to record without a stopwatch that measures elapsed time both ways. The objective is to fix the *when* and *how long* with a high degree of certainty.

USE OF SYMBOLS AND ABBREVIATIONS. All symbols, abbreviations, and illustrative devices must be fully explained either in the text that describes the chart or somewhere on the chart as a legend.

LAYOUT SKETCHES. One or more layout sketches of the individual work areas should be prepared and attached to the chart for reference purposes.

MULTIPLE ACTION ELAPSED TIME SUMMARY. The chart should be completed by the addition of a concise summary that shows the actual, and percentages of, time utilized for all subjects covered. A comparison of present and proposed arrangements, if required, should appear on the proposed chart as well as in the PMR's final report.

How Multiple Activity Charts are Used

In certain types of operations, one or more members of a working force are often waiting for other members of the force, or in a workshop situation, either the operators or the machines are not fully occupied during the operating cycle. The nature of the operation may be such that the operator or the machine might as well not be there. A common

example of this idle time syndrome occurs in machine work, when the machine automatically makes a cut under power feed with the operator standing by with nothing to do until the end of the cut. Then the machine is idle while the operator goes to the storeroom for a new cutting tool or a drawing.

The same condition occurs in many other kinds of operations, such as those carried out in government offices in which documents are the principal medium that requires time-consuming activities and processes. Whenever an operator and/or a piece of work are temporarily under the complete control of a machine or whenever the operator must wait for another operator to complete his task, idle time occurs, and the possibility of a procedure or method improvement exists. In the interest of effective production, it is necessary to minimize the amount of idle time.

The first step in undertaking the elimination or reduction of idle time from an operation cycle is to determine the following exactly:

1. What idle time elements are involved
2. When and where the idle periods occur
3. What causes them
4. How long they last
5. What relation each element has to other elements performed by the same operator, as well as to elements performed by other operators in the work force

This may be shown clearly by construction of a Multiple Activities Chart showing side-by-side all elements performed by all operators and/or machines involved.

CHECKLIST OF THE REQUIREMENTS OF A SYSTEMATIC METHODS AND PROCEDURES STUDY

In the preceding topics of this chapter, attention is focused on the use of standard forms and charts for recording M&P information as presently existing and on how changes might bring about improvements. Particular emphasis has been placed on the disclosure through systematic analysis of the following: (1) purpose, (2) place, (3) sequence, (4) persons, and (5) means.

The phrasing and content of the subrequirements and questions in the *Checklist of the Requirements of a Systematic Methods and Procedures Study* are intended to produce *blocks of information* that the PMR can easily relate to what was said earlier about analytical techniques through the use of the various M&P analysis forms. A high degree of selectivity is needed in coming to grips with the principal improvement areas chosen as candidates for potential change. With practice, the PMR will develop the essential skills for

focusing on high-priority areas for such change and will be able to make his oral and written presentations to the RS increasingly productive.[1]

---

[1]It is beyond the scope of this guide to cover the many methods and procedures improvements that can be achieved through the application of *value analysis.* Value analysis, which is sometimes referred to as *value engineering,* is best characterized as the systematic application of a process that identifies a *function,* establishes the cost and/or relative contribution of that function, and explores alternative ways in which its elements may be provided at the lowest possible cost with no loss in required performance. This process differs from most other cost reduction processes by being *function oriented.* It involves a searching review of the functions of a product or system, as opposed to merely seeking lower costs in the production of the same result. The researcher who may be interested in further study of this subject should start with the United States Department of Defense's training guides, entitled *Principles and Applications of Value Engineering,* and *The Management of Value Engineering Programs*—Revised Edition. Washington, D.C., U.S. Government Printing Office, 1968.

CHECKLIST OF THE REQUIREMENTS OF
A SYSTEMATIC METHODS AND PROCEDURES STUDY

1. *Purpose of the Operation and the Procedure Involved*
   - Why is the operation performed?
   - What is accomplished? Is it necessary?
   - Must it be performed at this point?
   - Could it be combined with a preceding or subsequent operation?
   - Does the operation produce a product that satisfies the requirements of all users or only a few?
   - Do the results obtained justify the cost?
   - Can the product be purchased at a lower cost?
   - Can the purpose of the operation be performed better in some other way?

2. *Quality of Output*
   - What, if any, are the standards as to grade or quality of output for this operation?
   - Has full information on the nature, purpose, and enforcement of all operating standards been provided?
   - Who checks and enforces the standards?
   - How are the standards of quality checked?
   - Are output inspections perfomed at the critical point or at the completion of the operation?
   - Can operation and inspection be combined?
   - Are quality requirements established by users of the output or by subsequent process steps?
   - Should standards of quality be improved or are they higher than required by the following steps in the process?
   - Are those concerned informed regularly and fully on how well they meet established standards and productivity goals? (i.e., feedback)
   - Can changing the requirements of preceding or subsequent operations simplify this operation?
   - What are the principal reasons for rejects or waste loss?
   - Can quality of job be improved by using new processes?

3. *Material and Supplies Required* (forms, products, etc.)
   - Are present material and supplies and/or information sources suitable for the purposes for which they are being used?
   - Can cheaper materials and supplies be used?
   - Are the material and supplies being used furnished to the operation in the most economical condition as to shape, size, quantity, accessiblity and uniformity?
   - Could the material and supplies be modified in order to improve the operation or output?
   - Would improved inspection of incoming materials and supplies eliminate subsequent process delays or waste losses?
   - Can newly developed materials, supplies, or equipment be used to advantage?
   - Are the material and supplies used to the best advantage during the present processes?
   - Is the source or preceding operation performing any unnecessary work?
   - Is the use of material and supplies properly measured and controlled to insure maximum economy and still meet operating requirements?
   - Can the number of material and supply items be reduced through standardization?

4. *Material and Supplies Handling*
   - Does the source deliver materials and supplies directly to the first processing point?
   - Are incoming materials and supplies conveniently located in order to eliminate rehandling and delay?
   - Could electric or manually activated office machines be used to advantage?
   - Is the use of a conveyor justified?
   - Can gravity chutes or roller conveyors be utilized to deliver incoming or completed work?

- Is a storeroom efficiently located and stocked?
- In storage or production operations, would the use of pallets and forklift trucks improve the handling procedure?
- Can any other form of mechanical handling be substituted for manual labor, such as hydraulic, electric, or air hoists?
- Would improved communication between source points and processing points improve operations?
- Can operations be combined in one work area to reduce material, supply, and document handling?
- Can materials and supplies be purchased in a more convenient size or design to facilitate processing and handling?

5. *Tools and Equipment*
- Is the presently used equipment too large or too small for the tasks performed?
- Can two or more pieces of equipment be combined to serve the same purpose?
- Is the equipment obsolete?
- Would the purchase of more modern equipment be justified by cost or quality of the output?
- Can material or forms be fed and removed from the equipment more quickly?
- Is the equipment being operated at maximum efficiency consistent with safety and quality of output?

- Is preventive maintenance work on the equipment regularly scheduled and performed?
- Does the output volume justify the development of special work aids?
- Is the equipment properly designed to accomplish the purpose for which it is being used?

6. *Working Conditions*
- How is the work assigned?
- Is the work prescheduled for the employees?
- How does the worker obtain necessary work aids such as reference sources, the latest rate schedules, regulations, supplies, etc.?
- Could a less skilled employee handle the "make ready" chores?
- Are the materials, tools, and equipment properly pre-positioned?
- Is the work area properly laid out to produce the desired results with the least physical and mental effort?
- Are conditions good for ventilation, light, and heat?
- Can smoke, dust, and fumes be reduced or eliminated?
- Is the work area noisy?
- Have safety measures, such as operating rules, been published and are they enforced?

CAN YOU ADD TO THIS CHECKLIST? (IF SO, DO SO.)

EVALUATION OF OPERATING METHODS CHANGES

The dynamics of operating methods change are illustrated dramatically by a government agency that introduced a central correspondence dictating machine and a transcription pool. The following considerations were given special attention:

1. Physical arrangements had to be made to place a signaling device and a microphone on or by the desk of each official who would be served by the centralized dictation system.
2. Instead of enjoying the relative independence that comes with being assigned to only one official, the transcribers (typists) were transferred to a new organizational unit (pool) and were required to work together under one supervisor instead of separately.
3. Duties were changed to the disadvantage of the transcribers because in their former positions their pay was augmented, since approximately 28 percent of their time had been devoted to secretarial and receptionist duties. Their salaries were not changed, however, though replacements when needed were hired at the lower rate for a typist.
4. Having a private secretary had become a status symbol with agency officials. Being deprived of this in the interests of alleged increased efficiency aroused opposition.
5. The new transcribing center was deliberately, but temporarily, overprovided with typists, in order to remove all ground for complaint that the new transcription service was less efficient than the old system.

This particular innovation actually increased and speeded correspondence replies by approximately 35 percent and reduced transcription costs by about 20 percent. It clearly demonstrated that changes that are carefully planned and that adequately anticipate reactions are usually successful and that those most affected adjust quite rapidly. Indeed, after a month of efficient service, they frequently expressed a preference for the new system.

Deterrents to Successful Change

Despite the previously described success, there are many changes that have an opposite effect. Unsuccessful implementations of change are usually traceable to the following conditions, some of which are unavoidable:

1. Changes that call for new work demands on long-tenured workers and require knowledge or skills they cannot achieve
2. Changes in groupings of established cliques, in relationships with a long-respected supervisor, or with friends or changes that bring together old enemies
3. Changes in the real or assumed standards according to which individual or group performance (production) will be appraised.
4. Changes that involve the possibility of new recruits being paid at a lower rate for identical work as compared with those transferred from other positions without loss of pay

Assuming that a new system has been requested and is based upon a carefully simplified procedure or that mechanization will result in less drudgery, overtime, bottlenecks, and other unwelcome inefficiencies, a capable PMR soon comes to recognize the signs of adverse reaction on the part of RS personnel and plans his implementation work along the lines suggested next.

Requirements for Implementing Methods Changes

There are no established or all-inclusive rules for implementing operating methods changes, but the following are considered to be minimum requirements:

1. The new operation (including the procedure steps, methods, etc.) should be written briefly with careful attention to clarity and should show each staff member what his contribution to the total effort is expected to be.
2. The explanation should anticipate as many as possible of the questions that will be asked, especially those affecting work hours, new skill requirements, learning-curve expectations, where to go for further information, what will happen if redundancies develop, and whether adjustments will be considered if exceptional situations occur.

Some adverse reactions on the part of RS supervisors may also be anticipated when new or revised operations are introduced. Most good supervisors have developed strong views on the work standards that can, and should, be achieved in the organization under their direction. All such attitudes, however, must go by the board if the changes are to be made. Part of the adjustment will come automatically, when it is realized that conditions prevailing under the old system no longer exist, but there will remain a latent tendency to appraise the new arrangement in terms of what is most familiar. Many new operations suffer from the lack of an impartial or enthusiastic attitude at the outset. The PMR must therefore be ready to collaborate with supervisors in the development of new performance standards. When called upon, he/she also should advise on the kind, amount, and form of control information that becomes the new *output criteria* of the operation.

Special Considerations in Implementing Operating Methods and Procedures Changes

There is no absolute standard by which M&P improvements can be evaluated, but there are a few basic considerations. One or more of the following considerations should exist in any change intended to improve operating efficiency or reduce operating costs:

1. *Increased effectiveness* in the context of M&P means that a static staff (in numbers) becomes better able to deal with a workload increasing in size. It is best achieved by cutting out work found to be unnecessary, in the sense that it does not contribute directly to achieving the mission of the organization unit concerned.

2. *Saving paper and time* is most often achieved through the redesigning of printed forms and by adjusting procedures so that two or more officials (or units) share the same copy of a form or extract from the same copy the information that they need for their own purposes.

3. *Improvement of work area layout* is accomplished by studying the flow of work involved in the principal procedures of an organization, relocating the main work areas to reduce the distance between centers, and thereby reducing the total distance traveled and the time required to transport work-in-progress. A secondary consideration in improving work area layout is the amount of space allocated to each of the staff involved in the system. Experience has clearly demonstrated that supervisors tend to regard the amount of space that they, personally, or their area of supervision occupies as a status symbol. It is worth noting in this connection that floor space can be conserved in a number of ways that will help to give the appearance of spaciousness and, in other ways, will make more usable work space in rooms and on desk tops. For example, if shelving for office forms and supplies is designed to accommodate specific items, instead of being all of one size and distance apart (vertically), approximately 45 percent of the shelving space for office supplies can usually be made usable.

4. *Service to direct supervisors* takes the form of providing them with the essential know-how of systems improvement work and the *time* to make the detailed review of present workload and methods, in order to design improvements that will result in better performance. In general, the PMR will find his greatest opportunity in the following areas:
   (a) Eliminating procedural deficiencies
   (b) Developing operating standards according to which the supervisor can appraise operating performance
   (c) Designing work planning techniques, such as schedules that give advance notice of probable bottlenecks, the need for shifting staff, or securing authorization for temporary assistants or overtime work
   (d) Proposing training ideas that both inform the staff what is expected and how it is to be accomplished, referring them when necessary to sources of additional guidance in connection with new operations, unusual situations, or when substituting for another staff member

5. *Ideas designed to assist supervisors* may take many forms because they have general responsibility for achieving the mission of the organization. The most important and easily identified operational area of assistance to overhead supervisors is in the improvement of management information and controls that signal the existence of exceptional (especially) and general conditions calling for direct action from the supervisory level of the organization. This assistance need not be confined to information on damaging departures from the normal but should provide a sound basis for decisions that will augment positive operations trends and permit corrective action when negative trends become apparent.

6. *PMR service to the organization* may be of any kind that results in a reduction of effort, confusion, cost, and the like, but those operations which have the greatest organizational impact are in

the form of departmental, divisional, etc., consolidations; mergers of positions; and meeting the need for specialized staff. Organizational consolidations tend to occur more to achieve needed cost reductions than to improve operations; therefore, opportunities for rendering organization-wide service tend to be more limited than opportunities in the other areas briefly summarized previously. This should not be a cause for discouragement. Bringing parts of an operating process together that were previously separated, eliminating unnecessary work, and taking the drudgery out of it, make work easier and allow all personnel to get home or to recreational activities on time.

The appraisal of new operating methods and procedures, then, is an essential part of public management research. Good operating methods are not ends in themselves, and sooner or later management will turn its critical spotlight on all activities that do not make a *direct* contribution to the achievement of organizational goals. This is to say that PMR studies must be conducted so that they acquire tangible values to the organization the research center serves, even if there are seemingly insurmountable difficulties in attaching a monetary savings to that kind of effort and achievement. In these circumstances, it is well for the PMR to keep some sort of record of his achievements, with estimated values expressed in terms of man-hours, earlier availability of outputs, or in any other terms that reflect an *operational benefit*, even if it cannot be measured as a direct monetary saving.

Chapter 7

RESEARCH REPORTING

A PUBLIC MANAGEMENT research report should be a forthright presentation of factually accurate information, in narrative and illustrative form, that sets forth simply and logically what the researcher did to fulfill the T/R of a research assignment. In this sense, a research report can be characterized as a *communication document.*

While this chapter is not intended to provide the ground rules for achieving more perfect literary exposition, it is clear that many research reports suffer because those who write them often have too little knowledge of sentence and paragraph structure and often are not aware that grammar and punctuation were invented to facilitate the expression of thoughts and understandable descriptions of events and arrangements.

RESEARCH REPORT FUNCTIONS

The principal functions of a research report include the following:

1. An immediate effort to *establish rapport* between the researcher and the reader, by a clear statement of what research problem has been attacked, and the implication of whatever setting prevails.
2. Presentation of *relevant data*, both fully and understandably, with sufficient explanation to substantiate all interpretations and conclusions reached by the researcher.
3. *Interpretation* of data in the light of their implications for resolution of the research problem with which the report is concerned.
4. *Summarization* of conclusions and recommendations made throughout the report with any proposals concerning ways to implement recommendations or the direction of additional research.

TYPES OF PUBLIC MANAGEMENT RESEARCH REPORTS

Meaningful interim, final, implementation, and postimplementation reports are the most effective way to keep research sponsors (RS) appraised of the status of a public management research project, and enthusiastic about its end results. With these objectives in view, good reporting becomes the essential communication link between the PMRC and its research sponsoring affiliates.

This chapter does not assume that research reports should be written in precisely the same fashion. It abhors stereotyped, sterile, mass-produced pieces of public management research reporting that could drain the lifeblood from professional endeavor. There is ample opportunity for creative thinking and writing in the public management research process. This does not mean, however, that the *conventions* of basic composition can be disregarded. They are discussed at length in many manuals and therefore are not given much space in this guide.

While not strictly a convention, *organization* is essential if the researcher's time and effort are to be used wisely and if a report is to be balanced, factual, and interesting. *Discipline* is the crux of the long labor of sifting authorities, investigating the many and varied processes and procedural steps, and adding one's own critical comments only after these have been fully assimilated.

The form, content, frequency, and circulation of research reports should be covered in the T/R and the work schedule. As indicated in the preceding chapter, however, decisions on these matters should be based upon the PMRC's professional judgement of RS information needs and discussions with RS personnel. The following is a summary of the types of research reports that have been found most appropriate in public management research reporting.

Interim Research Reports

Interim or progress reports are usually made in medium- and long-range research projects, but seldom in those requiring less than one or two weeks to complete. They may be presented to the RS in various forms, depending on the informational needs set out in the T/R. They might include, for example, graph representations, written statements concerning the work so far completed in accordance with agreed upon work schedules, conference memoranda, or an oral presentation that may be supplemented by a written summary of the conferences or staff meetings at which oral presentations were made. Written interim report format can range from tabulated listings of research topics, to detailed write-ups explaining the status and tentative conclusions concerning each phase or step of the project.

An interim report may contain varying *amounts* of information depending upon the scope and duration of the assignment. The following, for example, would be appropriate to indicate:

1. What topics within the assignment have been completed (against the research project schedule)?
2. What interim benefits or conclusions have been tentatively identified?
3. What will be done in researching the next topic or topics?
4. What assistance or approval is required to accomplish the next phase of the project?

Unanticipated problems, such as a deterioration or withholding of RS personnel cooperation, might be mentioned as one way of focusing attention on such matters. This is especially appropriate if the interim report is oral and if attendance at the presentation conference is confined to key officials. This use of interim reports also assists in the *timely* recognition and resolution of unforeseen problems and restrictions that could hinder or even prevent the successful implementation of recommendations (if any) considered relevant at this particular phase of the project. Regardless of its form, content, and timing, the PMRC has a continuing responsibility to confirm in writing any discussions, agreements, and conclusions relevant to the assignment.

Although an interim report usually provides the best opportunity to communicate matters of mutual interest to the RS, it is desirable to circulate copies of interim reports and notes on what happened at any RS conferences. Copies should be circulated (usually on a confidential basis) to those selected by the RS. It should be recognized by all concerned that research-in-progress may be of a confidential nature and that report distribution should be the responsibility of the RS liaison official or, alternatively, the official who initiated the research assignment.

Final Research Reports

The final research report, which could in some cases be the only tangible output of a research project, should be regarded as the major communication link between the PMRC and the RS. Normally, a written report supplements, or is supplemented by, an oral presentation.

The types of assignment and the needs of the RS should determine its length. For example, a short *report letter* may be used in situations in which the assignment consists of a simple gathering, digesting, and presenting of factual material on a single topic. Usually, however, the breakdown of a subject into several topics requires a more comprehensive treatment. For example, a more lengthy report might consist of a fairly detailed discussion of findings, the methods employed in the research, and the tests applied to ensure data validity.

Final reports can also be *formal*, in the sense that established authorities and reference resources are quoted at length, rather than employing statistical summaries. It should be remembered, however, that results are usually achieved by *implementing*, rather than merely *communicating* information and discussing methodology. Accordingly, a final research report should not contain more than is necessary to convey essentials.

Final Report Objectives

A final report issued by the PMRC should, as a minimum, do the following:

1. Quote in its entirety the T/R.
2. Summarize the work performed as it relates to the scope indicated in the T/R and in any subsequent modifications or extensions.
3. Summarize the findings in a clear, logical manner, together with any supporting assumptions.
4. Recommend a future course of action, if so stipulated in the T/R, including, where appropriate, a proposed implementation strategy and listing of (suggested) future research work in priority sequence.
5. Serve as a continuing reference document for

RS use in any training or orientation conferences and for reference purposes in any post-evaluation effort. This includes a suggestion for a year or later audit of actions taken as a result of the research project.

Final Report Format

The so-called *long form* report is usually used to present final submissions of research findings, and any recommendations prompted by them, only if so required in the assignment T/R. The principal elements of such a report should be the following:

1. A *cover* that includes the name of the project used throughout the report; its number, if a numbering system has been adopted by the PMRC; the name of the RS organization for which the research project was undertaken, the month and year that the report is submitted, and the full name of the PMRC. All this information can be typewritten on a two-by-four-inch label or imprinted on plastic covers if sufficient copies are being issued to justify this expense. Less expensive covers are available and serve the purpose just as well, especially the use of a transparent plastic front cover or opaque plastic front and back covers.

2. A *title page* that should contain the same information as appears on the outside cover, with the optional addition of the following:
   (a) The names of those who participated in the project
   (b) The names of those to whom copies have been *officially* provided in accordance with prior agreement with the RS

3. A *copyright* is usually highly recommended in the cases of scholarly research and reports that might be quoted with or without permission. Application should be made to the Copyright Office, Library of Congress, Washington, D.C. 20540. Notice of copyright is required by law, preferably on the page following the title page.[1]

4. An *executive summary* is also an optional inclusion intended to save time for executives who might otherwise delegate the task of summarization to an unqualified or less interested subordinate. It should be in the briefest possible terms, outlining the scope of the research assignment, its findings, and the conclusions reached. In appropriate cases, a proposed plan for implementation and/or an indication of the need for additional research on the subject of the report or related subjects should be mentioned, both in this summary and later in the main body of the report.

5. A *table of contents* that lists each principal subject and topic covered under each subject heading, using the same designations as those used in the body of the report. The page number should be entered opposite each subject and topic title.

6. A *preface* should not be a summary but should contain informative statements on the following matters in sequence:
   (a) The *background* of the assignment, such as information on the date the project was initiated and the T/R was adopted. This may be quoted in full, or parts extracted that cover enough to establish the official nature of the project.
   (b) The *research method employed*, specifying the library research resources used, interviews conducted, on-the-job inspections of work centers made, and any other library or field research work performed.
   (c) *Acknowledgments* in which appropriate credit is given to those who have been of special assistance in the fulfillment of the research project or who have authorized the quotation of their statements or the use of their data. Some research center directors give staff recognition by listing their names and titles on either the report title page or on a separate page, such as immediately preceding the table of contents. The name and title of the official who initiated the project and the RS liaison official should also be mentioned.
   (d) A *synopsis of report coverage* should not duplicate the executive summary referred to previously but should cover essentially the same information from the standpoint of the topics covered. This is usually in the nature of a summary of the *research areas* explored, any *problems* encountered, and a definite but not overly enthusiastic indication of satisfaction with the main body of the report that follows. One sentence about each of the principal subjects researched is usually quite sufficient in an introductory statement of this kind. It will help the reader if the subjects are treated in the same sequence as they are reported in

---

[1]Copies of *The Copyright Act of 1976* and regulations issued by the Copyright Office are available from the Superintendent of Documents, United States Printing Office, Washington, D.C. 20402.

greater detail in the main body of the report.

7. *Findings and conclusions* should make up the main body of the report. Findings contain the details on what was researched, and they are the basis for the conclusions and/or recommendations derived from the research effort. Remarks should be confined to statements of fact in all discussions of findings, and all conclusions should be identified as arising from those facts and/or the consensus of authoritative thinking about them. If recommendations are appropriate, they should be fully documented and explained. It is generally useful to divide the main body of the report into topical sections reflecting the different areas covered by the research work.

All recommendations should show how, if implemented, they will improve the effectiveness of operations, such as the delivery of public services or improved community or interorganization relations. Suggestions should be in broad terms and provide for a logical and orderly course of action. The usefulness of the final report will be enhanced if the researcher identifies the means and the steps necessary to assure that appropriate action is taken.

8. An *appendix*. If exhibits such as schedules and graphics, or lengthy quotations, etc., are not essential to the body of the report, they should be placed in an appendix. Placed there also may be supportive material such as photocopies of particularly important documents, financial and statistical tables, maps, and photographs.

9. A *bibliography* serves the twofold purpose of providing the reader with guidance concerning available literature on the subject of the report and demonstrates that the researcher is familiar with the existing literature. It is frequently of assistance to the reader if *classics* in the field of the research are identified either with a symbol, such as an asterisk or a brief notation concerning their author's contribution to that field. Bibliographic material should be classified according to the topics discussed in each chapter of the report. It is usually preferable to arrange bibliographic citations in the following manner:

    (a) Author's surname, first name, and any initials
    (b) Coauthor's surname, first name, and initials
    (c) Title of the book or document (including edition number, if any, beyond the first edition)
    (d) Publisher's name
    (e) City and state of the publisher's location
    (f) Year of publication

10. *Minority views* are sometimes included in team-produced research reports. In the event that RS personnel have had a *major* part in carrying out the research assignment, it may serve a useful purpose to provide space in the final report for a minority statement that focuses attention on specific findings and/or conclusions about which there is a lack of agreement or on the relevance of factual material and its interpretation. Space should be allowed for this only if reasons and explanations for alternative findings or conclusions are provided by the dissenters.

To summarize, the overall requirement for writing a final research report is to provide prospective readers with a document that is at once organized in thought and logical in its structure. While there are many variations in report arrangements, the essential test should be—is it apparent to the reader what the researcher has attempted to accomplish, and is it organized so that the logic of presentation becomes apparent through a casual inspection of the table of contents or perusal of the text?

The following is a typical *Table of Contents* of a final research report that explores one or more management hypotheses:

Chapter   *Topic and Subtopic Titled*

I. THE PROBLEM AND ITS SETTING
    1.1 The problem and any subproblems
    1.2 Hypotheses
    1.3 Delimitations
    1.4 Definition of Terms and Abbreviations
    1.5 Assumptions
    1.6 The Need for the Research Project
    1.7 Organization of the Report
    1.8 Acknowledgments

II. REVIEW OF RELATED PUBLICATIONS (if any)
    2.1 Prevailing Interest in Theoretical Concepts
    2.2 Measurement of Interest
    2.3 The *Smith Approach*
    2.4 The *Jones Approach*
    2.5 Summary of Prevailing Interest

III. RESEARCH METHODOLOGY AND PROCEDURES
    3.1 Data Collection Procedure
    3.2 Data Processing Procedure
    3.3 Assessment of Research Methodology and Procedures

Follow-up Reports

Follow-up reports deal mainly with developments that occur after the acceptance of a final research report. They are often specifically called for in the T/R but are also sometimes requested later by the RS in its effort to determine the following:

1. What progress has been made in fulfilling assignments by its own personnel for further research or in implementation of recommendations or changes that were suggested in the final report?
2. What developments have occurred that might have an impact on RS operating policies and long-range plans?
3. What, if any, new developments have occurred that might result in the application of new technology or the utilization of previously unused informational resources?
4. What developments have occurred in other public organizations that might be applied within the RS organization or by joint endeavor?

It is appropriate that such follow-up research work should be covered by a T/R that cites earlier research work and spells out what is to be undertaken *now* in relation to that *earlier* effort. The format and content of the follow-up report may be essentially the same as that outlined in connection with final reports, and a later discussion in this chapter dealing with oral reports.

REPORT DRAFTING GUIDELINES

There is a direct relationship between the *method* of fulfilling a research assignment and its resulting *reporting requirements*. The omission of reporting considerations from the assignment, especially in a final report, can result in either excessive time incurred in data collection activity or inadequate time provided for the collection of data essential to the proper development of a compelling presentation of findings. In correcting the latter deficiency, misunderstandings with the RS can result, especially at the later stages of an assignment. It is, therefore, essential to consider certain, often neglected, reporting requirements in fulfilling all research assignments.

Reader Viewpoints

Reader viewpoints, especially those of persons known to have extensive familiarity or emphatic views on the subject matter of the research project, must be considered. Furthermore, the expected readership may include many persons who may be directly affected by the conclusions and recommendations. Since these parties may hold differing views, consideration must be given to both groups in drafting the report, bearing in mind that those directly affected by it are often in an excellent position to influence the opinions of those in authority whether to accept or reject its conclusions. It follows, therefore, that the PMRC should always attempt to present its reports in a positive way, stressing desired improvements and resulting benefits, rather than in a critical way, which would put RS personnel on the defensive.

Selectivity

Selectivity refers both to the amount of *detail* to be included, and the need for selective *emphasis* on certain points. This is a key consideration in drafting research reports. For example, the researcher should recognize RS background in the subject matter of the report, the current organizational climate, and the degree of preliminary RS acceptance of the PMRC as an agent of change and be impartial in criticism and/or praise.

Report Arrangement

Report arrangement should not be confused with the points discussed in chapter 5 that deal with line and staff organizational arrangements. As the term applies here, *arrangement* refers to the techniques employed in the preparation and presentation of subject matter in a way that will achieve the maximum reader impact. There are so many satisfactory report arrangements that it would not serve a useful purpose to review them here, except to stress the essential elements of report design as follow:

1. *Sectionalization*, as the name implies, stresses the point that the body of a report is easier to read and understand if it is divided into logical sections, each dealing with a separate research topic. An additional advantage is that it permits two or more members of the research team to write contributions to the report simultaneously.

2. *Emphasis* refers to the stress, through the use of appropriate adjectives and adverbs, to be placed on the salient points of each section. One way to do this is to employ italics, but a more subtle way is to provide a brief introductory statement, such as is used in news stories, to each section of the report, summarizing its coverage and identifying where that section fits into or is important to the overall *message* of the report.

3. *Headings* are for the convenience of the reader, not the researcher, except, of course, as an aid during the report writing process. After that, it is usually desirable to break up the narrative only as much as will contribute to reader understanding. This may be accomplished by the use of topical subheadings, subsections, or other breakdowns such as those arrangements illustrated in this guide.

4. *Exhibits* need not be confined to listings, tabulations of fiscal and other statistical data or to pictures. Exhibit material, such as facsimiles of printed forms or checklists or salient points in support of a particular research finding, is useful but should be included only to the extent that it will enhance reader understanding. If it is felt that narrative summary of the data in statistical tables providing extensive detailed support for a point of view cannot be achieved, then there is no alternative but to include the tables themselves. The critically important consideration in any such data presentation exercise is that the data be presented as *evidence for the conclusions* the researcher draws from them. In many cases, when the data is so extensive that it makes understanding difficult, the illustrative or tabular material should be in summary form with the details relegated to the appendix.

5. *Research findings data* are obviously the most important elements of any research report. It is generally best to separate the several subtopics into individual chapters, but if this results in a report that is so extensive it will repel rather than attract reader interest, there is no alternative but to group closely related subtopics into as few topical chapters as practicable. Each such chapter should conclude with, first, a brief summary that clearly establishes what has been reported and, second, state in what ways the findings are related to the overall research topic and the previously reported subtopic findings. Included here should be some indication whether the data presented supports or weakens any hypothesis that has been stated in either (usually both) the research proposal or the T/R. In either case, it will be found that restating the hypothesis that is being researched will strengthen the continuity of the discussion of the data and, thereby, make easier reading and more complete reader understanding.

In all cases in which research data is subjected to statistical analysis, the rationale for the employment of a particular approach should be indicated. For example, it is often critically important for the reader to know not only that a particular correlative technique has been employed but also *why* it has been employed. It is generally a very worthwhile idea to keep in mind that the *why* of research reporting is generally equal to or more important than the *what*.

6. *Interpretation of data* in a casual manner can do more to defeat the purpose of management research than almost any other shortcoming in the research process. Researchers frequently conclude, often without being aware of it, that having once presented their data in graphic and narrative form, they have done all that is needed. It is not the discussion and display of data that is important; it is the *interpretation* of it that is the basic reason for the whole research process. When one asks *what*, *who*, *when*, and *where*, attention is thereby focused on the most elementary aspects of a condition. It is only when one is presented with data and required to explain *what it means* that he/she is called upon to exercise a higher mental process. Without inquiry into the full *meaning of research data*, there can be no resolution of the research problem to which it relates.

ORAL PRESENTATIONS OF FINAL RESEARCH REPORTS

Success in achieving acceptance of a PMRC's findings and conclusions may well depend upon a forceful and well-prepared oral presentation at a RS conference. To succeed in this type of presentation, a thorough knowledge of subject matter, confidence in the validity of the research team's findings, and enthusiasm for its conclusions are the principal ingredients. In addition, a successful oral presentation requires the following:

1. Careful presentation planning and an agenda that leads the listeners from one salient finding or conclusion to the next
2. An ability to understand those to whom the presentation is made, including knowledge in advance of the number and background of the listeners
3. An ability to transmit ideas in a clear, logical, and concise manner
4. An ability to hold the audience and keep the presentation or conference moving toward a mutually satisfying conclusion
5. An ability to respond to questions and statements during or at the end of the presentation, including calling upon research team members to contribute to the presentation by explaining topics or points that they have had a part in developing

The utilization of RS managerial personnel, as well as research team members, in making the final oral report presentation should be considered. Visual aids, such as handouts, blackboards, overhead projectors, motion pictures, models, as well as recordings and field trips to inspect the site of operations about which conclusions and recommendations are offered, add greatly to oral presentations. Frequently it will be found that the employment of these and other audiovisual aids will allow the PMRC to treat research topics in greater depth, particularly in areas where some management officials lack a full understanding of the implications of research findings, conclusions, and proposals concerning the implication of any recommendations.

REPORT PITFALLS

If certain pitfalls are avoided consistently, a research report's readability will be improved. Among the things to avoid are the following:

1. Long, involved sentences
2. Long paragraphs
3. Unnecessary technical terms, phrases, and obscure terminology
4. Complicated statistical tables in the text of the report
5. Excessive reference to exhibits, whether in the text of the report or in the appendix, and to citations to authoritative publications
6. Single spaced typewriting with narrow margins

Similarly, worthwhile improvements will result if the following suggestions are adopted:

1. Include *significant* figures *extracted* from exhibits in the body of the report, with explanations of their relevance to the conclusions they support.
2. Utilize *ratios* or percentages that are usually more easily comprehended than comparisons of actual figures.
3. Cite specific examples to illustrate the relevance of particularly important statements.

EVALUATION OF RESEARCH REPORTS

The most critical difficulties bearing on the results of public management research result from the *quality* of the research work performed. It is always an aim of research to produce as high quality work as possible within resource, schedule, and technical constraints. It is important, therefore, that reports come to grips with aspects of quality in the performance of research work so that any necessary corrections may be initiated. A checklist of the kinds of questions that should be asked when assessing the quality of a research report includes the following:

1. Have the validity and reliability of evidence presented in the report been systematically established and described?
2. Did errors of fact come to light in staff reading of the report?
3. Were appropriate methods selected in the search for and analysis of the data?
4. Were adequate provisions made for establishing all conclusions concerning the need for control over operational variables?
5. Were data validity test results properly conducted, interpreted, and applied?
6. Are there specific changes in report content, format, or style that should have been made to improve its effectiveness?

While the term *quality* is applicable to all research work, it is not subject to precise definition. Questions such as these provide a means for allowing persons not directly involved in the research process to offer constructive suggestions on the conduct of the assignment. While it may be true that outsiders cannot judge the quality of research work without expertise, it is also true that many characteristics of public management research are common among diverse programs. These common features provide a basis for mutual respect for technical competence.

An analysis of the reasons why sponsors either reject or fail to utilize the result of research reveals several *content deficiencies*. The following should serve as a warning to researchers that the RS expects more than a mediocre product:

1. An obvious lack of new or original thinking on the subject.
2. Report content suggests it was prepared on the basis of a diffuse, rambling, superficial, or unfocused research plan.
3. Demonstrates a lack of understanding of already published work in the field, as reflected in references to, and in the treatment of, the pertinent literature.
4. Reveals a lack of background and experience in the essential methodology of social research.
5. The PMRC appears uncertain about the future directions research on the subject should take.
6. An absence of acceptable scientific rationale.
7. Lacks sufficient statistical detail and contains an uncritical approach to the use of the statistical material it does include.

This chapter has discussed several forms of research reports. The best way to acquire an appreciation of the nature and the several forms of such reports is, first, to become thoroughly familiar with the concepts and guidelines outlined in this chapter and, then, to inspect a representative sample of reports issued by prestigious organizations, such as the National Institute of Health; the Brookings Institution; the National Association for Public Administration; The Conference Board (of New York); and the many learned societies, professional associations, and occupational/trade organizations. The government publications are generally free or nearly so, while others may carry a charge that usually amounts to little more than the cost of printing, handling, and postage. All of them demonstrate, to a greater or lesser extent, the essential characteristics of the kinds of reports that managements, both government and in the private sector, have come to expect and are accustomed to use in the decision-making process.

Chapter 8

RESEARCH CENTER
AND RESEARCHER EVALUATION

PUBLIC MANAGEMENT *performance* is not the recording of a series of events, each of which can be evaluated in a similar manner across different environmental and institutional settings. If *problem solving* is accepted as a fundamental applied research activity, then performance is quite simply *success in solving different types of problems in different environments*. While it is necessary in the short run to try to develop new, and to refine accepted, techniques for indicating perceived success in solving management problems, taking into account the perspective and circumstances of the perceivers, a start should be made toward classifying management problems and problem-solving approaches in different environments. As the word is used here, *environments* refer to the conceptual and material technological and institutional settings in which public management problems occur.

The measurement of performance in PMRCs, therefore, calls for an understanding of how different research solutions are produced. To improve the quality of these solutions, the evaluator must know how they were reached and for what purpose they are required. This involves a detailed and systematic study of how knowledge is created through research activity. This, in turn, requires investigating what researchers do to identify and represent problems and what researchers do to select and apply research strategies and tactics to their solution. It also involves the study of the interrelationships between ideas,

both technological and social.

A review of the study given during the past several years to research performance criteria clearly shows that the emphasis has been on a search for a pragmatic and simple basis for allocating *research rewards* and not necessarily on strategic and tactical contributions to problem solving. It has been demonstrated, for example, that the often used *number of reports* criterion tends to defeat systematic and equitable evaluation of research performance because, when this becomes known, researchers are inclined to spend a considerable amount of time writing up research they would not otherwise consider for publication. They, therefore, spend correspondingly less time on actual management situation analysis and management problem solving.

Similarly, the use of criteria such as the number of innovations proposed and/or accepted are less than satisfactory, because their understanding necessitates an extensive consideration of important factors, such as the *relevance* of the subject matter, the *quality* of the reports as sources of authoritative information, the *depth and breadth* of coverage, and perhaps most important of all, the *use* to which findings can be put for socially beneficial purposes.

The following subsections of this topic provide a basis for evaluating the overall performance of government research centers, as compared with *basic* research centers, individual research supervisors, and the researchers that they supervise.

OVERALL RESEARCH CENTER PERFORMANCE INDICATORS

The *Government Research Center Capability Indicators* provide a list of thirty-six factors that are suitable for evaluating public management research program performance and capability on an overall basis. The list covers the essential categories of performance indicators without dwelling on variables (i.e., between research organizations as well as research projects),

such as rates of change over short and long periods of time, the output goals of the organization, and relationships between public management executives and their research center colleagues.

The Government Research Center Capability Indicators list is intended for use as an approximate *score card* on which one inserts numbers representing both

GOVERNMENT RESEARCH CENTER CAPABILITY INDICATORS

A. *Productivity*
1. Number of research project requests received
2. Number of research project requests accepted
3. Number of research projects rejected
4. Ratio, acceptances to rejections
5. Number of interim research reports issued
6. Number of final research reports issued
7. Number of final research report pages (including exhibits)
8. Projects undertaken in response to "repeat" requests
9. Number of innovations proposed
10. Number of innovations accepted and implemented
11. Number of innovations accepted but held in abeyance
12. Number of innovations rejected
13. Ratio, innovations accepted to rejected
14. Number of project schedules overrun
15. Aggregate days of project schedules overrun
16. Amount of additional expense attributable to project schedule overruns
17. Amount of expense reduction attributable to project schedule underruns
18. Research center budget overrun/underrun at end of last budget coverage period

B. *Research Center Resources*
1. Adequacy of library collection
2. Adequacy of information retrieval system
3. Use of library by nonstaff
4. Research environment

5. Adequacy of interlibrary exchange arrangements

C. *Personnel*
1. Number of senior (professional) researchers
2. Number of journeyman researchers
3. Number of research support staff (including artists, draftsmen, photographers, copy editors, etc.)
4. Training in research methods provided to staff
5. Training in research methods provided outsiders (including research interns)
6. Aggregate "score" of all researchers based on the periodic researcher evaluation exercise
7. Average "score" of all researchers based on evaluation exercise

D. *Other Research Center Capability Indicators*
1. Guidance on research matters provided other research centers
2. Newspaper and journal articles/stories published on separate research projects
3. University/college evaluation of research program generally
4. Executive evaluation of research program generally
5. Professional society evaluation of research program generally
6. Participation in "parallel" research projects with other research centers

SUGGESTED ADDITIONAL CAPABILITY INDICATORS?

measurable factors and objective evaluations, for example, on a scale of 10 to 0, with 10 representing the highest possible *score*. The resulting overall *score* becomes meaningful when

1. It is used to compare, through *repetitive* evaluation exercises, performances over an extended period of time, such as annually for five years;
2. Any new, additional indicators are not allowed to distort the evaluation results by giving more or less weight to those previously used; or
3. Each successive evaluation exercise is used as the agenda for discussion on how the research center's performance and capability can be improved.

It will be observed that most of the capability and performance indicators are mainly *objective* in character, and relate to situations that are capable of improvement through managerial action. There are some, however, that can be quite subjective and call for searching out the causes that result in an adverse performance or capability *score*. The opinions of executives who utilize the research center and universities that, through report exchange relationships, are in a good position to evaluate the research work as competitors and as professionally qualified observers are cases in point. Nothing very much can be done, however, to qualify the evaluations of a research center's overall performance by such outsiders.

A word of caution is in order. The use of subjective criteria by the research center itself in its own self-evaluation may be useful as long as the results are for *internal use*. Their use for interorganization or interdepartmental comparisons introduces a whole series of variables that, between organizations, are virtually impossible to define in ways that are interorganizationally equitable. A considerable effort has been made, especially since the late 1950s, to formulate a set of performance indexes that can be applied to all research situations. This effort has produced only one example in which, with a significant expectation of success, an interorganizational comparison could be attempted. In that case a performance study was made in connection with exactly parallel research by several widely separated research centers under a government financed, privately executed series of research contracts. Even in this unusual situation, the comparison had to be limited because of *differences in approach* to the research problem and substantial differences in manpower applied by the several research centers.

RESEARCH MANAGEMENT CONTROL

A realistic definition of research management control is a system that provides management with the tools for determining if a research project is progressing toward its goals and for determining the extent and causes of any goal deviations. The multiobjective nature of public management research projects encounters immediate obstacles in the attempt to design and implement such a system. In most management research programs, the *final* course to goals is frequently not among the approaches originally selected.

Irrespective of the difficulties encountered, certain primary requisites must be considered in the development of even the most modest of research management control systems.

Performance Standards

This first requisite consists of finding appropriate *benchmarks* from which to measure deviations from research plans. These are usually expressed in terms of cost of time, materials, services, and overhead expenses such as art and duplication work that are calculated and presented according to a more or less standard (for the particular research center) format.

By comparison, even in routine industrial-type research work, management control standards present problems because standards are relative, rather than absolute. Nevertheless, it is usually fairly easy to establish standards for production work compared with the complexities inherent in *research* projects. Productive standard hours, yield rates, loading cycle times, and other frames of reference are not adaptable to research activities. It follows, then, that management control of research must develop its own set of standards that, in the absence of precise measures, can be tentatively used as *benchmarks*. These must be gradually refined until they become sufficiently accurate for use in estimating the main budgetary, manpower, and information resource requirements of similar research projects.

Each exercise in project cost analysis can be made to contribute to the collection of *benchmarks*. In time, it becomes possible to estimate as much as 80 percent of project costs with a high degree of accuracy, to allocate overhead costs on a pro rata basis between projects, and arbitrarily to distribute the remaining costs on a pro rata basis among those expense classifications that have already been credited with known and overhead costs. With experience, the imperfections of this cost allocation system will be reduced, and to that extent the standards used for project estimating and control purposes will be more perfect. One should not expect that they will ever be completely perfect, but if they serve to reduce estimating errors and identify budget over and under runs, thus leading to more error-free systems of overrun prevention and control, the system will have justified the time-consuming and inherently experimental exercise involved.

Performance Accountability

The adoption of performance standards implies accountability for time, materials, etc., costs. Production employees, especially supervisors, have had years of experience with performance control methods and procedures. They have come to accept them for their benefits to their employers and themselves. Only in relatively recent years have engineering designers and research managers been made generally aware of budget processes and the use of *standards* in estimating project costs. There is still a long way to go in gaining acceptance of the idea that research project managers should be accountable for their use of research manpower, equipment, materials, services, and any other categories of expense-related items. Research performance control methods will not improve or gain full use, unless research managers insist on more complete and realistic project planning and plan adherence. In the meantime, it must be conceded that the environment for establishing effective individual and organizational attitudes on positive accountability is not nearly as favorable as it is in industrial production programs.

Reporting

The third requisite of a realistic research performance control system calls for ability to include all specified data relating to the operational variables being controlled. These routine processes involved in the collection and summarization of operating data present no conceptual difficulties, particularly when electronic data processing technology is utilized. Once the required kinds and amounts of operating data are in hand, the reprogramming of automated data processing equipment should generally, but not always, cause fewer difficulties in research implementation and reporting than in complex industrial production situations. It should be recognized, however, that individual researchers are more involved in providing direct information inputs to the control system than the industrial production worker, where many of the data input tasks are fully automated.

It has been demonstrated that, ideally, researchers should be required to report only a minimum of essential data relating to the status of their work. In the research environment, especially, every effort should be made to avoid the imposition of excessive requirements of management oriented data at the working level. This may not produce as much variation in the coverage of computer assisted research management control reports, but they will gradually become more useful if the computer assisted input process is kept simple at the outset and improved or extended gradually until it is an indispensable research management tool.

Project Performance Evaluation

The fourth research management control system requisite is a capacity for research center performance evaluation, which can be characterized as a comparison of plans and results, together with an interpretation of all significant deviations. In research, this process is usually resolved at the team or center-wide level because of the difficulty of making judgements on individual performance after-the-fact on the basis of even the accurate and complete reporting described previously.

While it is held by some detractors of research management control that the problems inherent in the evaluation process are more troublesome than the establishment of the research plan, it should not be assumed that the evaluation of research performance is impossible. It must be conceded, however, that too little progress has been made to claim unequivocable success, but it does not follow that useful results cannot be achieved in the interest of improved research management control. For example, later in this chapter, a proven system for evaluating the performance of individual researchers and research supervisors will be introduced. Until a better device or refinements are provided, the sum total of the scores assigned to research program participants should be an acceptable researcher evaluation system requisite.

Corrective Action

The fifth requisite of a research management control system is a means for instituting corrective action, once the need for it is verified through comparisons of plans and research team performance under those plans. The techniques for corrective action are so many and varied that it is unproductive to try to select between them. In most situations, the *time-dependent* factor is most easily assessed but may not prove to be the most important for corrective action purposes. Lack of skill in the use of research resources, interruptions of work in progress, delays in getting approval of adjustments in T/R, mechanical breakdowns, etc., can be important deterrents to meeting deadlines and introduce other productivity evaluation pitfalls.

Follow-up Action

Finally, when corrective action is initiated, the control system should provide a way for information on the results of that action to reach the PMRC's management. *Feedback* is important, because management must have a way to choose between alternatives such as the application of increased or reduced research resources, a modification of project objectives, a change in the basic research plan, and the assignment of more staff, including specialized research capability. Feedback of this kind is lacking in most research management control systems, but improvements have been shown through devices such as subjecting past project performance reports to study and reassessment, formulating project models for staff conference use, and examining completed research work assignments to detect any deficiencies in the methods employed or the skill of the researchers involved. There are many other symptom identifying factors, but the foregoing are sufficient to demonstrate the kind of feedback that is needed.

Conclusion

If the foregoing approach to improved productivity is employed, attention should be focused at the outset on the careful definition of research objectives in each project as a whole, and then the project should be subdivided into successively smaller increments of work. Of particular importance is the consideration that research work is essentially creative in method and choice of areas of emphasis and priority. These capabilities are not easily subjected to qualitative or quantitative evaluation, unless they are closely identified with project and subproject objectives. With experience and experimentation, however, it becomes increasingly easy to draft task objectives that may be set forth in research work specifications (i.e. T/R), together with estimated costs, schedules, research specializations to be employed, and the criteria that will be used when the project is completed for evaluation and management control purposes.

RESEARCH STAFF PERFORMANCE EVALUATION

The *Researcher Performance Evaluation* is for the use of the research team or project supervisors in assessing the performance of the individual researchers assigned to them for instruction, guidance, and supervision. It is entirely *subjective* in its design and purpose. It is also largely self-explanatory because the qualities assumed to be essential may be weighted according to their importance in a meaningful researcher performance evaluation. To this end, the Researcher Performance Evaluation may be used in its present format or made more comprehensive by adding qualities such as appearance, public relations capability, and others. A more realistic score can also be achieved by assigning a weight to *each quality* to reflect the management view of their relative importance.

For example, there may be a consensus or management view that dependability, knowledge of research methodology, and productivity are the three most important qualities a researcher should possess. In that case, they might, in the order of their importance, be assigned the weights of 1.8, 1.5, and 1.3, respectively, with the other qualities being assigned lesser weights ranging from .5 upward to 1.0. By multiplying the weight assigned to each quality title by the number checked in the row of boxes following each quality, the product thus calculated may represent the number of *points* the researcher received for that quality. The sum of the points would be his overall *score* or his performance *grade* for the reporting period.

The results of this individual researcher evaluation

RESEARCHER PERFORMANCE EVALUATION Part One

Researcher's name	Supervisor's name	Date

INSTRUCTIONS:
Rate the researcher by placing an "X" in the box which most nearly expresses your judgement of each performance quality.

1. PERSONALITY: How does he affect his co-workers and task supervisors?
   ► Makes an exceptionally good impression | 5 | 4 | 3 | 2 | 1 | 0 | Unfavorable impression

2. MOTIVATION: What is his apparent point of view toward his research work?
   ► Very enthusiastic | 5 | 4 | 3 | 2 | 1 | 0 | Shows little enthusiasm

3. DISCIPLINED APPROACH: Approaches assignments in an orderly way?
   ► Always | 5 | 4 | 3 | 2 | 1 | 0 | Seldom

4. DEPENDABILITY: Is he dependable with respect to fulfilling his research assignments?
   ► Highly dependable | 5 | 4 | 3 | 2 | 1 | 0 | Not dependable

5. ABILITY TO FOLLOW IDEAS: Does he show an ability to follow ideas concerning his research assignments?
   ► Shows exceptional ability | 5 | 4 | 3 | 2 | 1 | 0 | Shows little ability

6. ATTENDANCE AND PUNCTUALITY: Does he attend regularly and is he punctual?
   ► Excellent | 5 | 4 | 3 | 2 | 1 | 0 | Indifferent

7. SKILL IN ASSIGNMENT FULFILLMENT: What are his assignment supervision needs?
   ► Requires only general instruction | 5 | 4 | 3 | 2 | 1 | 0 | Needs continuous guidance

8. SELF-RELIANCE: Is he an accomplished "answer finder"?
   ► Demonstrates superior initiative | 5 | 4 | 3 | 2 | 1 | 0 | Needs continuous guidance

9. PRODUCTION: Does he meet your quality and quantity standards of productivity?
   ► Demonstrates a high standard of productivity | 5 | 4 | 3 | 2 | 1 | 0 | Low productivity

10. ORIGINALITY: Does he demonstrate originality in his analysis of research problems and solutions?
   ► Exceptional originality | 5 | 4 | 3 | 2 | 1 | 0 | Very little

11. PROTECTIVE OF CONFIDENCES: Does he protect the confidences placed in him with respect to information entrusted to him whether or not he is advised on its confidentiality?
   ► On all occasions | 5 | 4 | 3 | 2 | 1 | 0 | Unreliable

12. REPLACEABILITY: Should he leave the organization for any reason, how great a loss would this be?
   ► A serious loss | 5 | 4 | 3 | 2 | 1 | 0 | Insignificant loss

13. ABILITY TO COLLABORATE WITH OTHER RESEARCH STAFF MEMBERS:
   ► Collaborates well | 5 | 4 | 3 | 2 | 1 | 0 | Shows little aptitute for collaboration

14. REPORT WRITING ABILITY: Does his reporting measure up to the organization's standard?
   ► Demonstrates excellent report writing ability | 5 | 4 | 3 | 2 | 1 | 0 | Needs training

PLEASE COMMENT ON THE FOLLOWING:

15. What especially commendable qualities are posessed by this researcher?

16. What suggestions can you make for this researcher's improvement?

17. How would you characterize this researcher's overall growth and progress in research skills?

Part Two

18. Please list the functions, activities and projects in which this researcher has been involved, and then place and ''X'' in the box which most nearly expresses your judgement on each quality.

Activity, projects, functions, etc.   Demostrated overall skill levels

a. _______________________________ High level | 5 | 4 | 3 | 2 | 1 | 0 | Low level

b. _______________________________ High level | 5 | 4 | 3 | 2 | 1 | 0 | Low level

c. _______________________________ High level | 5 | 4 | 3 | 2 | 1 | 0 | Low level

d. _______________________________ High level | 5 | 4 | 3 | 2 | 1 | 0 | Low level

e. _______________________________ High level | 5 | 4 | 3 | 2 | 1 | 0 | Low level

f. _______________________________ High level | 5 | 4 | 3 | 2 | 1 | 0 | Low level

g. _______________________________ High level | 5 | 4 | 3 | 2 | 1 | 0 | Low level

h. _______________________________ High level | 5 | 4 | 3 | 2 | 1 | 0 | Low level

i. _______________________________ High level | 5 | 4 | 3 | 2 | 1 | 0 | Low level

j. _______________________________ High level | 5 | 4 | 3 | 2 | 1 | 0 | Low level

k. _______________________________ High level | 5 | 4 | 3 | 2 | 1 | 0 | Low level

NOW PLEASE GO BACK OVER THE ENTIRE LIST OF EVALUATION QUALITIES AND CIRCLE THE NUMBERS OF THE FIVE ITEMS WHICH WERE MOST IMPORTANT TO YOU IN MAKING YOUR JUDGEMENT ON THIS RESEARCHER'S PERFORMANCE. PLEASE DELIVER THIS FORM TO THE DIRECTOR OF RESEARCH.

exercise may be used in connection with periodic salary reviews, promotions, and transfers and also in connection with evaluations of research center performance. They can also be used advantageously in career counseling that includes conferring with research center personnel on their individual weaknesses and strengths.

The aggregate *score* of the entire researcher staff and the average *score* based on a periodic researcher evaluation exercise might be included in the overall evaluation described in the preceding subsection and provided for under *personnel* in the Government Research Center Capability Indicators that are illustrated earlier in this chapter.

In the consideration of individual performance evaluations it would be useful to include the ideas of Douglas McGregor,[1] who advocated, in his now famous *Theory Y* approach to management, that responsibility for setting objectives and for the eval-

---

[1]McGregor, Douglas: *Leadership and Motivation.* Cambridge, MIT Press, 1966.

uation of progress in any type of organization be shifted to subordinates and that the foremen or supervisors act as advisers on the validity of goals and in the appraisal of objectives. This still controversial approach is characteristic of what is presently happening, to some degree, in the establishment of subobjectives in many management research projects.

McGregor's *Theory Y* goes a step further, by suggesting that higher *personal drives*, such as those relating to self-esteem and personal reputation, should be coupled with the objectives of the organization for the most effective accomplishment of a mission. Ineffective management control exists when operating personnel (researchers) look upon control as something primarily concerned with punishment, or merely as a *carrot-at-the-end-of-a-stick* technique. Effective research management control exists when research managers fully appreciate the difference between planned and actual performance. Where they do, research managers are in a far better position to institute control actions in areas of real public management importance.

INDEX